SELF-HELP SUPPORT GROUPS
FOR OLDER WOMEN

SELF-HELP SUPPORT GROUPS FOR OLDER WOMEN
Rebuilding Elder Networks Through Personal Empowerment

Lenard W. Kaye
Graduate School of Social Work and Social Research
Bryn Mawr College
Bryn Mawr, PA

Taylor & Francis
Publishers since 1798

USA	Publishing Office:	Taylor & Francis 1101 Vermont Avenue, N.W., Suite 200 Washington, DC 20005-3521 Tel: (202) 289-2174 Fax: (202) 289-3665
	Distribution Center:	Taylor & Francis 1900 Frost Road, Suite 101 Bristol, PA 19007-1598 Tel: (215) 785-5800 Fax: (215) 785-5515
UK		Taylor & Francis Ltd. 1 Gunpowder Square London EC4A 3DE Tel: 0171 583 0490 Fax: 0171 583 0581

SELF-HELP SUPPORT GROUPS FOR OLDER WOMEN: Rebuilding Elder Networks Through Personal Empowerment

1 2 3 4 5 6 7 8 9 0   B R B R   9 8 7

This book was set in Times Roman. The editors were Laura Haefner, Christine Williams, and Kathleen P. Baker. Cover design by Michelle Fleitz.

A CIP catalog record for this book is available from the British Library.
∞ The paper in this publication meets the requirements of the ANSI Standard Z39.48-1984 (Permanence of Paper)

Library of Congress Cataloging-in-Publication Data

Kaye, Lenard W.
    Self-help support groups for older women: rebuilding elder
networks through personal empowerment/Lenard W. Kaye.
        p.   cm.
    Includes bibliographical references.

    1. Aged women—United States—Social networks.   2. Social work
with the aged—United States.   3. Aged—Services for—United States.
4. Self-help groups—United States.   I. Title.
HQ1064.U5K4   1997
362.6—dc21   97-6368
                                                                                          CIP

ISBN 1-56032-461-9 (case)
ISBN 1-56032-462-7 (paper)

Dedication

This book is dedicated to my dear wife and friend Susan
and my wonderful children Lindsay Alison and Nicholas James

Contents

Acknowledgments

I wish to acknowledge the support of those individuals whose contributions served to make this project a success.

First and foremost, I am grateful to Elaine Pirrone, former senior acquisitions editor, and Bernadette Capelle, development editor, at Taylor & Francis for encouraging me to pursue this project, providing astute recommendations to strengthen the manuscript, and remaining most supportive and patient throughout the course of journey to publication.

I am also most grateful for the financial support of the AARP Andrus Foundation's Board of Trustees: Kenneth J. Cook, former administrator; Mary Louise Luna, former research associate; and Anita M. Stowell, research analyst. Additional financial support from the Bryn Mawr College Madge Miller Fund was instrumental in enabling the performance of follow-up data collection associated with the project.

I acknowledge as well the enthusiastic and talented members of the research team who so expertly performed the multitude of tasks and activities required of a project of this type. They included Veronica A. Neary, research associate; Rachael Peters, research coordinator; and Deborah Feingold, research associate. All three of these staff researchers worked tirelessly in the collection, interpretation, and organization of information about self-help support group activities both in Philadelphia and around the United States. Beth Michener performed all computer-processing tasks during the course of the research, and Joan Davitt contributed to the successful completion of the local field interviews with Supportive Older Women's Network (SOWN) members and facilitators as well as library research during the earlier stages of the project. Many thanks are due Susan Reisman, who took lead responsibility for follow-up data collection efforts associated with the project, including extensive library research and literature review tasks. Susan was instrumental in the development of many of the case vignettes found in the text. I thank as well a number of students and professional social work colleagues and specialists in self-help, group work, and gerontology who offered their own interpretations and perspectives on the self-help movement, the experience of older women, and group process. Included here are Jeffrey Applegate, Naomi Farber, Philip Lichtenberg, and Donna Tarnowski.

The cooperation and assistance of past and current SOWN program administrators and staff were instrumental in securing all necessary information about the organization, its participants, and the services provided. I sincerely thank Merle Drake, executive director; Ellan Rubin, managing director; Aileen Moleski and Jan Cooper, direct service coordinators; Valerie Chestnut, group facilitator; and Kathleen McCann, office manager. Merle Drake, the originator of the SOWN concept, truly represents one of the pioneers in older women's self-help programming in the United States. I also thank the various directors and expert staff associated with the innovative programs comprising the national roster of self-help support groups for older women for so freely giving of their time and expertise.

As has now become customary, members of the Bryn Mawr College and Graduate School of Social Work and Social Research community were most helpful in facilitating the administrative, budgetary, and technical execution of the support group study project. I acknowledge with thanks the support of Ruth W. Mayden, graduate school dean; Nona Smith, faculty grants officer; Thomas Warger, former director of academic computing; Carolyn Aspinall, public information writer/editor; Diane Craw, assistant to Dean Mayden; Adrienne D'Amato, former secretary to Dean Mayden; and Peg McConnell and Lorraine Wright, graduate school faculty secretaries.

Finally, I wish to extend my sincere thanks to those individual group members and facilitators of the SOWN program who so openly and honestly shared their personal and group experiences with the research staff. Without these women's gracious willingness to share the good times and the bad times in their lives with us there would be little here to report and share with others.

Contributors

Merle Drake, MS, is the founder and executive director of the Supportive Older Women's Network. She has been a presenter at numerous conferences across the country. She has also appeared on radio and television programs. She is the co-author of *The Power of Support: A Guide for Creating Self-Help Support Groups for Older Women.*

Andrea D'Asaro writes nationally distributed eldercare articles for working professionals who care for older parents. She also writes for women's and senior's publications on aging issues. Formerly a public relations professional, Andrea helped coordinate Older Americans' Month in Philadelphia and is active in the intergenerational movement to link older people with youth who can benefit from their wisdom.

Preface

Aging presents concerns for both men and women. However, as is so vividly documented by reports produced regularly by the American Association of Retired Persons' Women's Initiative (1994a, 1994b, 1994c, 1994d, 1994e, 1996a, 1996b), growing older constitutes a different experience for women in a wide variety of ways. Regardless of recent advances that have been realized in the economic status of elderly persons as a group, older women continue to be disproportionately affected by the adverse consequences of aging. Elderly women constitute a majority for every factor that places individuals at high risk of losing their independence through institutionalization.

Carroll L. Estes, director of the Institute for Health and Aging, University of California, San Francisco, and past president of the Gerontological Society of America and the American Society on Aging, has argued in convincing fashion that women's prospects for a satisfying old age are worse at every juncture as compared with those for men. In an address delivered at the July 1995 conference of the National Policy and Resource Center on Women and Aging, Estes reasoned that aging is a women's issue for a multitude of reasons, including the fact that although women live approximately 7 years longer than men, they are significantly more likely to be chronically impaired than their male counterparts, thus mitigating the benefits of greater longevity (Kleyman, 1995). Given older women's heavy dependence on Social Security benefits, Estes is critical particularly of recent congressional proposals to alter entitlement spending, including recommendations to make at least part of the Social Security system voluntary, to convert Medicaid into a state block grant program, and to introduce vouchers into the Medicare program. She feels that all such proposals are bound to weaken a system of economic support that is crucial in the lives of a large proportion of older persons generally and older women in particular.

Nancy Hooyman, professor and dean at the University of Washington School of Social Work, is also an articulate public spokesperson for the special demands of women's aging. She assumed recently the pro position in arguing that women, as compared with men, do experience more difficulties in old age (Hooyman, 1997). Hooyman reminded us that living longer does not necessarily equate with living better. Women's socioeconomic, health, and social statuses are documented as being significantly lower than those of men. The problems that are commonly associated with aging—such as inadequate retirement benefits, the burden of caregiving, and social isolation—are typically women's problems. And Hooyman predicted that women's health and economic concerns will increase in the future, in no small part because public policy in the areas of health and long-term care serve to perpetuate gender inequities, as do cutbacks in a variety of entitlements and benefits including Medicaid, Medicare, and Supplemental Security Income (Hooyman, 1997).

Women are more likely to live alone and reach advanced old age with chronic health conditions and limited financial resources (National Policy and Resource Center on Women and Aging, 1995; Villers Foundation, 1987). Especially at risk are those older women who are unmarried, live alone, and are African American or Latino (Commonwealth Fund Commission, 1988). And, of course, the population of older persons is growing at a feverish pace, and most of these persons are, and will continue to be, women.

The problems of aging are further complicated for women by the fact that they often outlive their helping network of family, friends, and neighbors. An older person's ability to remain in the community is threatened when there is an absence of social supports.

Social systems of support, defined as structured human attachments among kin, neighbors, friends, and members of voluntary associations (Gottlieb, 1981) may, in fact, be said to represent the largest form of health care in this country. Professional care continues to be the exception to the rule when it comes to characterizing the health care treatments received by Americans. In the context of aging, informal networks have been considered particularly crucial in providing a buffer against the negative consequences of aging. The benefits of intact and consistent social supports for promoting physical, social, and emotional well-being have, in fact, been well documented (Bear, 1990; Brody, Hoffman, Kleban, & Schoonover, 1989; Lee & Shehan, 1989; Wilson, Moore, Rubin, & Bartels, 1990).

Community programs that aim to reestablish caring, ongoing support networks for vulnerable older women experiencing multiple losses in their lives would seemingly represent a pivotal interventive strategy for enhancing quality of life. There has been a wealth of research into the characteristics of an older person's informal support network. However, there has been a scarcity of research, such as that reported here, that represents an in-depth, systematic analysis of the critical components of innovative community programs that seek precisely to reconstruct an older woman's social support system through self-help and self-care initiatives.

It is known from research findings that gender plays a powerful role in determining patterns of self-care in this country (Kart & Engler, 1995). Women tend to be more predisposed than men to treat their own health and mental health conditions (Kart & Engler, 1994), and they do so in a greater variety of ways (Rakowski, Julius, Hickey, & Halter, 1987). Other variables that appear to influence positively a person's engagement in self-help practices include age and education (Verbrugge, 1983, 1985), severity of disability (Norburn et al., 1995), race, levels of social support, socioeconomic status, and health status (Kart & Dunkle, 1989).

THE PROJECT

In light of the significance placed on self-care and natural helping networks for bolstering the personal lives of older women, the purpose of the project on which this book is based was to collect new and much needed information about the special benefits and drawbacks of formal organizations' efforts at social network building for older women. To this end, a two-tiered investigation was carried out that incorporated the following (a) a national review of a select group of model self-help support programs for older women throughout the United States and (b) an in-depth, personalized, community case study of a nationally recognized model program of self-help support groups, leadership training, networking, and community outreach education for older women.

Throughout the course of this analysis, *systems and networks of social support* are operationally defined as structured, ongoing human attachments for the purposes of physical and psychological well-being between older women and their relatives, friends, neighbors, and other significant relations. *Self-help delivery models* are defined as voluntary, small-group units that emphasize mutual aid and the accomplishment of a specific set of goals and objectives. As will be seen, program initiatives of this type emphasize personal responsibility, face-to-face social interactions, the provision of material and emotional support, and the learning of skills necessary to help older women function, ultimately, independently of professional facilitation.

The following specific questions formed the conceptual foundation for the project and guided the analysis of information that was collected:

- To what extent is the formal organization self-help delivery model succeeding in reestablishing a caring, ongoing support network for older women?
- To what extent does this type of program intervention increase older women's ability to cope with loneliness, stress, depression, and loss?
- To what extent does a formal program of self-help delivery encourage the establishment of an informal network of supportive relations between older women outside of the actual group meetings?
- How durable is the self-help delivery model for older women? That is, do such groups and interactions between members remain functional over extended periods of time?
- What is the optimal function to be served and responsibilities to be assumed by peer–volunteer leaders of self-help support groups?
- What types of self-help group strategies and methods are being used most frequently by those organizations that have undertaken such initiatives?
- Which specific self-help group techniques have proven to be the most effective or ineffective with older adults generally, and with older women in particular, in promoting self-help?
- What are the central characteristics of those older women who participate in self-help support networks?
- What is the requisite level of organizational resources needed for the mounting of an older women's self-help delivery model?

The answers to these questions will help give direction to the development of a comprehensive set of program development guidelines and best-practice methods for mounting self-help delivery projects geared to rebuilding older women's support networks in communities throughout the United States.

ORGANIZATION OF THE BOOK

Chapter 1 presents a brief overview of the current status of older women in the United States. Chapter 2 introduces the reader to a series of concepts central to the discussion, including social support, social networks, support groups, and self-help. In addition, Chapter 2 also explores the nature of the relationship between self-help and social support perspectives in their various forms. Having been introduced to the literature on self-help support groups and older women, the reader, in chapter 3 (written by Merle Drake and Andrea D'Asaro), is presented with a personalized, eyewitness portrayal of the historical evolution of the Supportive Older Women's Network (SOWN). Drake and D'Asaro's rich descriptive profile of SOWN sets the stage for the systematic and critical analysis of field material gathered during the course of the project and presented in chapters 4–8. Chapter 4 paints a sociodemographic profile of the older women and peer facilitators who participate in self-help delivery groups. This chapter begins with a description of the major methods and procedures that were adhered to during the course of carrying out the Philadelphia metropolitan area survey research associated with the project. Appendix A presents additional details concerning procedures followed for analyzing data and determining the extent to which the persons interviewed during the project accurately represented the views of all participants participating in the program. Chapter 5 provides an overview of the organizational and programmatic characteristics of older women's support groups, chapter 6 provides a similar overview in terms of the functional or process-oriented aspects of group activity and program operation, and chapter 7 considers the extent to which such groups make a difference in the lives of older women. Chapters 4–7 are based primarily on information collected from SOWN program group members, group facilitators, and staff. Chapter 8 changes gears and provides the reader with an appreciation for the kinds of self-help support group programs for older persons generally, and older women in particular, that are being carried out elsewhere in the United States. Chapter 9 provides the reader with an extended case study of an archetypal self-help support group for older women. It highlights a variety of issues that are likely to arise during the course of developing and maintaining the group. Chapter 10 then presents final thoughts concerning some of the major issues confronting older adult self-help group programming. Chapter 10 also attempts to tease out a series of recommendations for maximizing the efficacy of self-help group programming with older women. A listing of organizations, centers, institutes, associations, training programs and workshops, and specialized training materials for mounting and maintaining self-help group programs for older women and related individuals is found in appendix B. The reader is provided, where appropriate, with a brief description of each resource and the necessary information needed to make contact with or secure the resource.

Ultimately, it is the author's intention that the material presented in the pages that follow serve two equally important functions. First, the research-oriented reader should be provided with the necessary scientific evidence to assess the relative efficacy of self-help group programming for older women. Second, program planners and coordinators should be given access to the necessary practical and experiential information required to begin the process of conceptualizing and developing meaningful self-help support groups for older women. Both functions, it is argued, have been responded to inadequately by the literature that was available before this undertaking.

1

Aging and the Older Woman

The aging process and the changes faced in the latter years of life raise a broad array of concerns for men and women alike. Yet, the overarching significance of gender in understanding the aging process and the condition of old age has been repeatedly confirmed. Although men and women share a range of common experiences in the later years, women are significantly more likely to be affected by a variety of adverse repercussions as they grow older. Differences in the consequences of aging for women as compared with men extend to all dimensions of daily living. Women are more likely to live longer, be chronically impaired, become impoverished, live alone, and be widowed. The challenges that older women must confront arise from demographic, social, and physical origins.

An intimate understanding of the unique circumstances of aging and older women is essential to the conception and implementation of successful therapeutic interventions for this population. Regardless of the specific target population, many social programs and policies have failed as a result of insufficient or inaccurate knowledge of potential clients. There is no template for ideal service provision, only a requirement to provide as close to a custom fit as possible between the service offerings and recipients' needs. It is with this principle in mind that a brief review of older women in the United States is presented.

Naturally, it is imperative to understand that demographic and related data are, by nature, summaries that therefore present generalizations. Typically, there is as much variation within groups as between them. Nonetheless, such an overview does provide meaningful information on the characteristics of a representative member of the group at hand. It is a useful starting point for a thorough investigation of a more specific target client population.

In the case of self-help groups in particular, members are frequently self-selecting, gravitating to other people with common characteristics or concerns. Often, such groups evolve rather than result from deliberate planning. A significant number, though, are planned by lay leaders or professionals with the goal of attracting members with a shared purpose and thus require a solid foundation of client familiarity.

A PROFILE OF AGING WOMEN IN THE UNITED STATES

The definition of old age in the United States, often a somewhat random designation, has changed over time with increasing longevity and improved health status

1

throughout the life cycle. At any given point in time, this definition will vary, based on need or purpose, such as retirement or pension eligibility, senior citizen center membership, or Medicare eligibility. As life expectancy has increased, it has become more commonplace to refer to the young-old (65–74 years), the middle-old (75–84 years), and the old-old (85 years and older). It is commonly known that the elderly population is growing both in number and as a percentage of the total U.S. population. U.S. Bureau of the Census (1991) figures indicate that in 1990, 31.1 million Americans—12.5% of the population—were 65 or older. This number is projected to swell to 34.8 million by the turn of the century and to 68.5 million by the year 2050. Concurrently, there will be an aging of the older population, with the percentage of middle-old and old-old people increasing as the percentage of young-old people declines.

Women surpass men in life expectancy at birth by almost 7 years, with an average expected life of 78.3 years (United Nations, 1990). Differing mortality rates for men and women have resulted in a gender imbalance throughout later life, a discrepancy that is exacerbated over time. The 1960 ratio of 82 older men for every 100 older women will drop to only 65 men per 100 women by the year 2000. The sex ratio drops significantly as a cohort ages, with the old-old expected to consist of a mere 38 men per 100 women by 2000 (Atchley, 1997). Data from a U.S. General Accounting Office study have suggested that such demographic differences between the sexes affect their relative quality of life in old age. Women generally experience a lower quality of life on a variety of indicators including physical health, functional ability, perceived income adequacy, social contact, psychological distress, and cognitive ability. Differences are most startling regarding living alone and activities of daily living, with women clearly being the more disadvantaged (Haug & Folmar, 1986).

INFORMAL SUPPORTS AND LIVING ARRANGEMENTS

This gender disparity in old age is also closely associated with the presence and quality of an older person's informal network of family, friends, and neighbors who, in combination, must provide both functional and affective aid. In many cases, informal supports play an important role in supplementing formal service provision, whereas in others the informal support network is called on to substitute for an inadequate or absent formal system.

The Consequences of Living Alone

Although elderly men and women who live alone often live near their children or other family members and have frequent contact with them, those living alone lack informal support more often than do other older people. Elderly women are more likely than their male counterparts to live alone. Of elderly women, 42% live alone, compared with 16% of similarly aged men (U.S. Bureau of the Census, 1992b). Although approximately 75% of elderly men reside with their spouses, fewer than 50% of women live with their husbands and therefore are denied the functional, social, and emotional support derived from spousal cohabitation (Himes, 1992).

Women's increased longevity, as well as their greater susceptibility to widowhood, results in their predominating among those with living arrangements that entail a high dependency risk (Bould, Sanborn, & Reif, 1989) and a loss of social supports. The implications of reduced or absent social supports are significant. Choi and Wodarski (1996) reported that the presence of such aid tends to decelerate further deterioration of the aged person's health. Unfortunately, the research has indicated that the extent of social support is more likely related to the size of the available support network than to the actual need for care resulting from declining health, thereby eliminating guarantees of adequate assistance for many with serious need.

Family Support

Although both familial and nonfamilial informal supports must frequently work in combination to provide an adequate support structure for an aging individual, it is estimated that 80% of elder care is provided by family members. Every day in the United States, approximately five million people spend some time caring for a parent, a number that is expected to double within the next two decades (Nager & McGowan, 1994). As older women age, responsibility for meeting their escalating need for assistance is increasingly likely to fall to other women—usually daughters—who are aging themselves and comprise a seriously burdened source of social support. As a result, the typical caregiver is a married 45-year-old woman engaged in full-time employment (Nager & McGowan). The negative repercussions for both caregiver and recipient of weaving elder care into a brimming schedule of job, home, and other family responsibilities are significant.

Approximately 80% of elderly persons have a least one living sibling, dropping from an average of three among those in their 60s to just one for those in the 80s (Cicirelli, 1985). However, the availability of a brother or sister for support does not necessarily translate into actual provision of aid. Spouses and adult children comprise the first lines of support, with siblings called on secondarily. The role of siblings in the support network of elderly men and women is generally to provide a sense of security rather than to provide concrete assistance (Cicirelli, 1985). In actuality, fewer than 5% of elderly care recipients are cared for by a sibling (Bengston, Rosenthal, & Burton, 1990), with never-married sisters providing the majority of primary sibling care (Coward, Horne, & Dwyer, 1992).

Elderly Women as Family Caregivers

Elderly women themselves are frequently required to fulfill the role of caregiver to a dependent spouse. These caregivers, who are coping with the multiple stresses of aging themselves, tend to have low morale stemming from the burden of their support tasks. Aged wives caring for disabled husbands report an array of stresses, including the demands of constant care and supervision, emotional and physical hardship, reduced social contact, and anxiety related to financial concerns (Wilson, 1990). Female caregivers living with their husbands, as well as those with institutionalized partners, are highly susceptible to mild depression, loneliness, economic woes, and low life satisfaction (Staight & Harvey, 1990).

Many mid-life and older adults, roughly 551,000 persons, bear the responsibility of caring for their grandchildren. Sixty percent of these caregiving grandparents are women (U.S. Bureau of the Census, 1992a) who have responded to a variety of problems confronting their adult children, including emotional and mental health problems, drug addiction, alcohol abuse, and physical diseases, including AIDS. Although the benefits of intergenerational interaction are well documented, in many cases grandmothers do not desire the caregiving role at a point in their lives when their own aging—and perhaps that of a spouse—exert numerous demands. For others, a healthy and secure old age offers an opportunity to pursue a long-awaited change in lifestyle that does not include child care responsibilities. When neither parent is available or able to fulfill their familial roles, surrogate parenting by grandparents may take place. In 1990, 5% of children in the United States lived with grandparents with no parent present (Atchley, 1997). Parenting grandchildren takes its toll; most of those performing this function feel worried, tired, drained, and overwhelmed much of the time (Jendrek, 1992).

The Impact of Marital Status on Informal Support

At a time in life when social support, specifically that of a spouse, is particularly crucial, older women often find themselves newly single and, therefore, living alone and facing an immediate drop in their financial status. In addition to the prevalence of widowhood resulting from the respective longevity of men and women, unanticipated divorce in the latter years may place an older woman in a vulnerable position. Late-life divorce is distinctly different and, in many ways, a more challenging life event than for younger cohorts of women. As compared with their younger counterparts, older women are less apt to initiate the separation, are rejected from a partnership spanning half a lifetime or more, and typically renounce the possibility of remarriage. In addition, today's older women belong to a generation in which identity is closely linked to marital status and divorce is considered dishonorable. Older divorcees have a much smaller peer reference group, and therefore a lesser likelihood of crucial peer support, than do younger women. In combination with the consequences of the aging process for women, divorce further erodes the self-esteem of this population (Cain, 1988). The number of mid-life and older women who are divorced has grown over the past two decades as a result of an increase in the frequency of divorce in these age groups and fewer remarriages by women who are middle aged and older. In 1970, only 2% of women 65 years of age and older were divorced. This population grew to 6% by the year 1992 (U.S. Bureau of the Census, 1970, 1992b).

There are notable differences in the amount of emotional, social, and instrumental support received from family members by married and never-married older women. Presently married women, as well as those who have been married previously, receive more of all types of informal support than their never-married counterparts. The absence of both a husband and children contributes to the informal support deficits of aged women who have never married (Longino & Lipman, 1982). An older woman's marital status has financial consequences, as well. Unmarried older women frequently rely on Social Security benefits for 100% of their income. In 1990, 18% of unmarried female Social Security recipients 65 years of age and older had no other source of income, and for 33% it represented at least 90% of their total income (Grad, 1992). Given the multiple effects of marital status on aged women, it is not surprising that never-married women have lower self-esteem than other older women (Lee & Shehan, 1989).

Nonfamilial Informal Support

Nonfamilial informal support can confer social, emotional, and functional benefits to elder women. Informal supports are most commonly friends and social acquaintances but may also include clergy and neighbors, as well as formal service providers who surpass their official function to offer one or more types of informal support. Home health aides, social workers, and local merchants, among other formal service providers, may participate in the informal support network of an elder by providing social support or concrete assistance that is not integral to their formal or customary roles.

The multiple affronts encountered by many aging women emerging from widowhood, divorce, retirement, and prejudice generate special needs for friendships with others among their peer group, in particular (Jacobs, 1990). Research conducted by Adams (1985) concluded that frequent interactions with friends improved the psychological well-being of the older women studied. Although respondents typically identified old, nonlocal friends as their most intimate confidants, those nearby friends with whom they were emotionally close provided the greatest task-oriented support and were most important for their psychological health. The equity of friendships, as well as the availability of such social supports, plays an important role in the value of the relationship. Women age 65 and older who benefit from a relationship as much as their friend and those who give more help than they receive in return have higher morale than women who are primarily the recipients in a social dyad (Roberto & Scott, 1984).

Although close friendships usually become even closer with age (Bleiszner, 1989), the actual number of close relationships, with confidants in particular, tends to decrease concurrently (Babchuck, 1978). To compensate for the attrition in the friendship network resulting from retirement, ill health, and mortality, most older persons are steadily making new friends garnered from among acquaintances in the neighborhood, other participants in social and recreational activities, and present or past coworkers. The ability and propensity of older women, specifically, to acquire new friends has been documented. Adams (1987) reported that over a 3-year period elderly women not only replaced, but actually exceeded, the number of lost friends with new social relationships.

PHYSICAL AND MENTAL HEALTH

The consequences of ill health in the later years emerge from both the health profile of aged women and the impact of health care policy decisions on service provision and medical coverage. Also at work is the interplay between socioeconomic status and health. Not only are those who are old and impoverished more likely to suffer ill health, but for many there is illness-engendered poverty that arises as the result of health care costs that exceed an older individual's ability to pay (Grau, 1987).

A Health Profile of Older Women

Eighty-five percent of elderly women suffer from some type of chronic disorder, a higher incidence than among their male counterparts. In later life, women also experience more injuries and days of restricted activity and bed confinement than aged men (Hooyman & Kiyak, 1988). Although aged men are more likely to face life-threatening ailments and to need hospitalization, Verbrugge (1983) reported a higher rate of many types of chronic maladies for women, including arthritis, hypertension, the consequences of strokes, diabetes, incontinence, many orthopedic problems, and visual impairments. Heart disease and certain varieties of cancer are especially prevalent among older women. Heart disease is the primary killer of older women, and of women of all ages, and is more likely to be fatal among women than men. The root of this discrepancy is twofold: Women are typically older than men at the time of their first heart attack, and many of the tests designed to detect heart disease were developed for men and hence are less accurate when used to diagnose women (The Society for the Advancement of Women's Health Research, 1991). The most common cancer among women is breast cancer, with increasing age representing the greatest risk factor. By the age of 65, a woman's likelihood of having been diagnosed with breast cancer is 1 in 17, a figure that grows to 1 in 9 by the age of 85. Of those diagnosed with the disease, approximately one third will die as a result. Although breast cancer is the most common of all cancers diagnosed in women of all ages, lung cancer is the most prevalent killer of women of all types of cancers (American Cancer Society, 1992).

Those diseases that are traditionally less common among older women pose a special threat specifically because of their infrequency and subsequent low profile. The stereotype of persons who are HIV positive or have AIDS as predominantly male and young can have negative consequences for older women, specifically in the area of prevention. By the year 2000, there will be as many HIV-positive women as men worldwide. In addition, it should be noted that from the initial report of AIDS in the United States until 1989, the incidence of new cases among persons over age 50 increased 10% annually. From 1990 to 1992, the incidence of new AIDS cases among those 60 and older grew by 17%. Elderly women comprise a particularly vulnerable community as a result of several factors. Health care providers, like many in our society, assume that elderly women are not sexually active and are therefore unlikely to offer education on preventive measures. Because of misconceptions about what constitutes normal aging, many early symptoms of the disease are casually passed off as signs of old age, delaying treatment and precautions related to transmission (Wachtel & Stein, 1995).

Older persons suffer from a higher rate of occurrence of mental, as well as physical, disorders. The most common types of psychopathology observed in later life include depression, dementia, and paranoia (Hooyman & Kiyak, 1988). Depression, the most prevalent, afflicts more than five million persons over the age of 65, including 25% of older nursing home residents. Severe depression, that which requires professional treatment, is seen twice as often among women than men (Regier et al., 1988).

The Impact of Health Policies on Older Women

It has been suggested that the lack of adequate national attention to policies concerning the health of elderly persons—such as long-term care provision and financing, patient rights, prevention, and health promotion—is the result of the fact that the aged population in the United States is largely female. As women continue to be devalued in our society, issues particular to this population are accordingly denied sufficient attention. Policy decisions regarding health care for older Americans of both genders may also be negatively affected by societal attitudes toward elderly people. The belief that the value of a 60- or 80-year-old person's life is less than that of a younger person results in policies that limit or deny health care services, medical technology, and reimbursement to older adults (Friedman, 1993). Many health care industry analysts, however, have predicted that the aging baby boom generation will have a positive impact on the health care system and government lawmakers, increasing attention to menopausal issues such as heart disease, certain cancers, osteoporosis, and estrogen replacement therapy (Wachel, 1992).

Policies addressing the provision and quality of long-term care are of particular concern to aging women as long-term care is unquestionably a women's issue. In 1990, 75% of nursing home residents 65 years of age and older were women (Taueber, 1993). Further supporting the connection between long-term care and the concerns of women is the fact that the overwhelming majority of informal caregivers to the aged are female as well.

Health Care Coverage

In the United States today, the availability and affordability of health care may very well constitute the most serious problem confronting elderly people (Jorgensen, 1993). Given the physical and mental health profile of elderly women and the high cost of health care, the availability of comprehensive health coverage is critical. Yet, many women lack adequate health benefits in later life. Elderly women who have never been employed outside of the home or who have done so only occasionally generally have health insurance that is inadequate to meet their needs. Divorced and widowed women are particularly vulnerable as they are more likely than their married peers to have little or no private insurance (Hooyman & Kiyak, 1988). As a result of their lower socioeconomic status, as discussed in this chapter, older women are less able to pay privately for medical care not covered by a third party.

LABOR FORCE PARTICIPATION AND RETIREMENT

The changing profile of the American labor force has, and will continue to have, a significant impact on women of all ages. Demographers and industrial forecasters are in consensus regarding an aging civilian workforce in which increasing numbers of women and racial and ethnic minorities will participate (Barnum, Liden, & DiTomaso, 1995; Zultowski, 1995). By the turn of the century, women, minorities, and immigrants are projected to comprise the largest portion of the entering workforce (Buhler, 1992).

A Profile of Women's Careers

Not only will the numbers of older working women increase, but the nature of workers' careers over a lifetime will likely differ from those of earlier cohorts. As a result of increasing average life expectancy, improved health in the later years, and the escalating economic demands stemming from a longer potential period of retirement, extended and multiple careers will become more commonplace and the average retirement age will likely edge back toward 70 (Kirkland, 1994). The concept of "reengagement" has been proposed as an alternative to traditional retirement practices, particularly in light of changing economics and demographics of older Americans. Such a return to the working world might take the form of full- or part-time employment, mentoring, community service, or any combination of these options (Kouri, 1984). Many middle-aged and older women choose, or simply end up in, contingent work arrangements. Such labor force alternatives include part-time employees, independent contractors, temporary workers, on-call workers and day laborers, and leased workers. Although older women are slightly overrepresented in the contingent workforce, women of all ages are more highly represented in such alternative employment than are men. Whether contingent employment represents a choice or a default, such workers face lower wages, fewer benefits and legal rights, marred career paths, and diminished retirement security, shortages that are especially damaging to women in the potentially stressful years of later life (Employee Benefit Research Institute, 1994).

The Impact on Employers

Projections of an aging and increasingly female workforce have prompted preparatory action on the part of many proactive employers. The U.S. Office of Personnel Management, in a report titled *Revisiting Civil Service 2000: New Policy Direction Needed,* advised the redirection of managerial emphasis from recruitment and retention to effective management of the existing workforce. Specifically, the federal government is urged to commence a reengineering process that will include both motivating an aging workforce and aiding the advancement of women and minorities into the managerial and executive levels (Cameron, Jorgenson, & Kawecki, 1993). With the numbers of working women, dual-career households, single parents, and elder employees at all-time highs, many corporations such as Johnson & Johnson have introduced policies and programs to help employees resolve work and family conflicts and, concurrently, improve morale and productivity (Galen, 1993). A much smaller number of private sector companies, including AT&T, Eaton Corp., and Met Life, have formal programs to address specific concerns of aging women such as the impact that menopause can have on the companies' employees and, therefore, their operations (Rice, 1994).

Labor Force Conditions

Relative to White men, both women and minority group members are subject to lower wages, a disparity that increases with age when tenure, education, and skills are controlled for (Barnum, Liden, & DiTomaso, 1995). Conditions of discrimination and low pay are further pronounced in occupations segregated by sex. The effects of women's low earning status continue to take their toll into the retirement years, negatively affecting psychological, physical, social, and economic welfare (Perkins,

1990). Compounding the effects of lower wages is the lack of aggressive retirement planning by many women, often resulting in a state of economic insecurity in the retirement years (Perkins, 1992).

Finding themselves lacking the financial resources to enjoy a comfortable and possibly lengthy retirement, many older women return to paid employment to supplement their income (Perkins, 1990). Although it is clearly to the economic benefit of women to remain in or return to the labor force, older workers are likely to encounter several impediments. Age discrimination and negative stereotypes regarding work performance limit aged workers' ability to progress in their place of employment and in addition makes reentry unnecessarily difficult. Also, community resources designed to assist older workers in their job search and provide training and retooling are scarce at best. Societal norms further hinder the process of continued or renewed elder employment as the emphasis is typically on the disengagement of the older worker from the workplace (Rife, Toomey, & First, 1989). Women who have dedicated much of their adult lives to the home and family may find their homemaker role coming to an end as they enter mid- or late life as a result of divorce, widowhood, or disability. Often referred to as displaced homemakers, such women often seek new opportunities in the job market where they are confronted with a unique combination of barriers, even following participation in special career preparation programs. Challenges faced may include age and sex discrimination, inadequate job preparation and training, low self-esteem, a lack of confidence, and frequently unrealistic job expectations (Benokraitis, 1987).

Retirement

The impetus for retirement has a notable impact on retirees' adjustment and satisfaction. In this regard, there are gender differences in retirement conditions that render retirement adaptation processes different for men and women. A study of female retirees, primarily in lower and middle-level occupational positions, indicated that family needs are a critical factor in the decision to exit the workforce. These women tend to feel that they retired sooner than they would have liked and, feeling forced into a family-centered lifestyle, often experience adjustment problems (Szinovacz, 1986). Other research has supported findings that the timing of women's retirement is more frequently influenced by family needs than is the case for men's retirement (Vinick & Ekerdt, 1989).

ECONOMICS

Regardless of the well-documented advances that have been realized in the economic status of elderly persons (Maddox & Clark, 1983; Moon, 1985; Preston, 1984) the "feminization of poverty" for the aged in particular remains a harsh reality (Gonyea, 1994). The repercussions of economic hardship permeate many other aspects of the lives of older women. Financial instability, poor health and inadequate health care, inferior living conditions, and strained family and social relations interact cyclically, feeding into an increasingly inferior quality of life.

The Socioeconomic Status of Older Women

Older women have slightly more than half the income of their male peers, with respective median incomes of $8,189 and $14,548, resulting in a poverty rate of about 16% for women age 65 and older. Yet another 10% are classified as near poor. And the incidence of poverty among aged women increases with advancing age. Approximately 13% of women between the ages of 65 and 74 have incomes below the poverty level, a figure that increases to 20% for those 75 years of age and older. When viewed as a percentage of the total population of elderly poor in the United States, the ranks of women comprise a startling 71% (U.S. Bureau of the Census, 1993d).

The lower socioeconomic status of elder women, as compared with elder men, stems from a number of sources. Although the gender gap in wages has improved over time, year-round, full-time female workers of all ages earn just 71% of what men earn, a disparity that increases with advancing age. The comparable figure for the subgroup of women age 65 and older drops to 65%. As a result of lower paying jobs and little or no labor force participation, the majority of women still receive higher Social Security benefits as spouses than as retirees, a particular concern for never-married women who are more likely to depend on Social Security benefits exclusively. In addition, women are only half as likely as men to qualify for pension benefits, and those who are recipients receive approximately half as much (U.S. Bureau of the Census, 1993c).

Although there has been a "greening of the aged" among select subpopulations, others, notably widows and other women living alone, are among the most poor (O'Grady-LeShane, 1990). In 1992, the median annual income for elderly widows was $9,281. Statistics for the same year indicate that, among older women, 22% of widows, 27% of divorcees, and 37% of those separated lived below the poverty level (U.S. Bureau of the Census, 1993b). A comparison of income data for older men and women further emphasizes the financial disadvantage of women. Widowed and divorced women earned 75% and 76%, respectively, of the income of widowed and divorced men. The greatest disparity in income, however, occurred in the married category. Elderly married women earned only 44% of the income of similar-age married men (U.S. Bureau of the Census, 1991), largely due to the fact that married women are less likely to be in the labor force full time.

Davis and Rowland (1990) pointed out that over the next 30 years, the gap between elderly women living alone and all other persons will significantly widen. It has also been projected that by the year 2020, poverty among elderly people will almost exclusively be a problem of elderly women living alone (Commonwealth Fund Commission, 1987).

A Historical Perspective

The negative impact on older women's financial well-being of social policy decisions and the resulting structure of social programs is apparent in many cases. Without an understanding of the historical underpinnings of such decisions, the original intent may be perplexing or unclear. Although such an understanding does not improve the suitability of these programs to today's older women, it can aid in the development of a revised system to better meet the needs of current and future generations. Given elderly women's significant dependency on Social Security benefits, a brief review of this program's evolution is warranted.

Achenbaum (1986) addressed the disparity in the benefits of Social Security between men and women. From its inception, the Social Security Act of 1935 was based on several assumptions: (a) married couples need more financial resources than single people, (b) women will accumulate their own wage credits, and (c) traditional family values place women at home raising and caring for children. These assumptions regarding the employment status of women were challenged during World War II and again at the end of the war when women disappeared from the labor market to make jobs available for returning veterans. This inherent conflict in the assumptions regarding women and working status versus dependency obfuscates the objectives of Social Security. Do women receive insurance or welfare? Achenbaum noted that as late as 1952, only 36,000 women (2 percent of those over sixty-five years of age receiving benefits) were eligible for both spousal benefits and retired worker pensions.

However, not until the early 1970s did gender-specific issues related to Social Security benefits receive deserved attention. As a result of several Supreme Court cases it became apparent that the basic assumptions regarding women and work status were somehow in conflict. Achenbaum (1986) noted that the consequence of Social Security measures aimed at protecting people increasingly seemed at odds with existing regulations geared to providing equal treatment. The implications of these debates and conflicts are apparent in the lower economic status of elderly women who have become the direct heirs of these policies based on conflicting assumptions. They affect a large segment of the population, putting them at economic risk.

Rodeheaver (1987) traced the historical underpinnings of the economic status of women in terms of social policy. The traditional role of women as dependent greatly influenced the development of the Social Security Act of 1935. By popular conception, widows were considered part of the deserving poor. There is a resulting inherent assumption in social policy that, because of the dependency role of women, solutions to their problems belonged in the home and within the family. Rodeheaver highlighted historically the unwritten criterion for distinguishing undeserving poor women from deserving poor women by asking the question whether their poverty arises from their inability or unwillingness to remain dependent on a husband. Ironically, the current plight of aging widows living in poverty does not place them at a significant advantage.

There is considerable support of this view of Social Security policy. Abramovitz (1988) emphasized that the message conveyed is women who are proper and deserving women belong in the home. By encouraging them to remain in the home, social security unintentionally reinforced the economic dominance of men over women and regulated women's participation in the labor force in accordance with the productive and reproductive needs of patriarchal capitalism in the twentieth century.

ETHNIC AND RACIAL MINORITIES

The numerous adversities of aging affect minority women to an even greater degree than nonminority women as they face the triple jeopardy of being old, female, and of minority status. Although a relatively small percentage of the total aged population in the United States, the percentage of minority elderly is predicted to increase markedly over the coming years. The percentage of non-White elderly persons, 10.2% in 1990, is expected to climb to 15.3% in 2020 and to 21.3% in 2050 (Angel & Hogan, 1991). Although a very small percentage of the total elderly population (2.9%), Asian–Pacific Islander elderly persons represent the fastest growing group of elderly in the United States today (Tanjasiri, Wallace, & Shibata, 1995).

Data on African American and Hispanic elderly persons in the United States are relatively plentiful. However, the same is not true for aged members of other minority populations. As a result, detailed demographics on aged minority women specifically, as opposed to elders of both genders, are not readily available for all minority groups. As reflected in the following sections, data for both Native American and Asian–Pacific Islander women as a discrete subpopulation are scant. Clearly, this sounds a call to action for gerontologists, sociologists, and demographers in related fields.

Financial Status

Indeed, the impoverishment of elderly people in the United States is disproportionately a problem of African American and Hispanic women, particularly if they are unmarried (Ozawa, 1995). Whereas 14% of aged White women have incomes below the poverty level, 38% of African American and 25% of Hispanic women age 65 and older live in poverty. Minority women 75 and older have an even higher incidence of poverty: 43% and 32% for African Americans and Hispanics, respectively (U.S. Bureau of the Census, 1993d).

Within each ethnic and racial group, regardless of age, women are more likely than men to live alone (Commonwealth Fund Commission, 1988), whereas elderly African American women are the most likely to live alone of any group (Himes, 1992). Elderly women living alone, minorities and nonminorities alike, have the greatest risk of being poor. Fifty-eight percent of older African American women living alone and 50% of elderly women of Hispanic origin living alone have incomes that fall below the poverty level; the comparable figure for their White counterparts is 23% (U.S. Bureau of the Census, 1993d). In the event of impaired health, in particular, African American and Hispanic older women have fewer alternatives for living arrangements than do their nonminority counterparts (Woroby & Angel, 1990).

Given the lesser financial resources of elderly female minorities, housing costs present a significant economic strain, particularly for those living alone. In 1991, 11% of elderly Hispanic women living alone spent between 70% and 99% of their incomes on housing, and 30% spent at least half of their incomes on housing, making this population the most burdened by housing costs. Among African American women living alone, 24% spent half or more of their income on housing, slightly above the figure of 20% for aged women of all races and ethnic groups living alone (U.S. Bureau of the Census, 1993e).

Native Americans of all ages are more likely than nonminorities to live in poverty. Among the Navajos, for example, 47.3% live below the poverty level. More than half have no piped water or indoor toilet, and 46% live without electric lighting in their homes. The implications for the aged, particularly those who are ailing, are significant. For those who can no longer remain in their homes, the availability of reservation health facilities for elderly people, nursing homes in particular, is poor. Because of the paucity of such services, most Native American elderly persons in need of nursing home care must leave the reservation and their families, friends, and familiar surroundings. In non-Indian nursing homes, there are typically no staff who can communicate with Native American residents, no traditional foods, and no knowledge of or adherence to customs and cultural norms (Mercer, 1994).

In comparison to other minority elderly, Asian–Pacific Islanders fare quite well financially. Of men and women 65 years of age and older, 12% of Asian–Pacific Islanders have incomes below the poverty line as compared with 10% for Whites and 31.9% for African Americans. Elderly Asians living in married-couple families are more likely to have incomes in excess of $50,000 (27.6%) than are both their White (18.1%) and African American (10.4%) counterparts. However, statistics for all families with persons 65 years of age and older indicate that 10.1% of Asian–Pacific Islanders live below the poverty line as compared with 5.4% of Whites. This figure is not, however, as glaring as the figure of 22.4% for African Americans (Tanjasiri et al., 1995).

Employment

Women of minority status are also faced with significant disadvantages in the workplace. In 1980, 63.7% of African American women aged 55 to 59 worked as maids, food service helpers, and nurses' aides and in other menial positions; 56.3% of Hispanic American women worked in similar positions, but with fewer in service roles and more working as operators and laborers (Atchley, 1997). This cohort, now among the ranks of the elderly, collected lower wages during their years of employment, are less likely to receive pension income, and have lower Social Security benefits as a result of their higher concentration in the less economically desirable positions within the blue-collar sector.

Health and Mortality

Similarly, health concerns and mortality rates differ for aged minority women. Life expectancy at birth for African American women is 73.7 years, nearly 6 years less than for their White peers, whose life expectancy at birth is 79.5 (U.S. National Center for Health Statistics, 1993). On the basis of middle mortality assumptions, the U.S. Bureau of the Census (1993a) projected that, from the present to the year 2010, the discrepancy in life expectancy rates for African American and White women will actually grow slightly, while overall longevity for both groups will increase.

Although the discrepancy in life expectancy between African Americans and Whites decreases with increasing age, older African Americans of both genders have a comparatively higher incidence of illness and disability (Atchley, 1997).

The Native American population, too, is aging and suffering many of the ills of other minority counterparts. It is estimated that 71% of all Native Americans over age 60 have impediments to performing their activities of daily living and tend to have a higher than average rate of chronic illness and a shorter life expectancy.

For example, Navajos, the largest tribe in the United States, have an average life expectancy of 73.7 years (Mercer, 1994).

In contrast, Asian–Pacific Islander elderly persons have a lower incidence of all major diseases and have a lower proportion of self-reported fair or poor health status (versus excellent, very good, or good) than all other older Americans (Tanjasiri et al., 1995).

CONCLUSION

The aging process and the experience of old age for women in general and minority women in particular are riddled with unique concerns and challenges. As discussed in this chapter, the positive impact of social support and cohabitation on this population extends to the realms of physical and financial, as well as emotional, well-being. Regardless of the nature of the presenting life situation, the support and understanding of peers—other older women experiencing the same circumstances— is particularly critical to the welfare of elderly women. In the next chapter, formal mutual aid and support groups are discussed as they relate to the needs of aging and elderly women.

2

Informal Support Networks and Self-Help

Over the past decade, increasing numbers of gerontological researchers have sought to gain a better understanding of those factors that contribute to successful aging and positive mental health among older adults generally, and among older women in particular. More precisely, these investigations have attempted to determine what constitutes a high quality of life for the older adult. Chapter 1 introduced the many factors that influence the quality of life for aging and elderly women, often to their detriment. However, the research has consistently documented the positive influence of the availability and use of social supports by older adults, both in the normative aging process and to mitigate the deleterious effects of a broad array of special situations.

INFORMAL SUPPORT NETWORKS

Informal support networks or social supports may consist of any combination of family, friends, neighbors, and others whom an individual can depend on to provide assistance either with routine responsibilities or in the event of a crisis. The support provided may be emotional, social, or tangible, but all types have a positive impact on the recipient's sense of well-being. When the support role is reciprocal, the benefits accrued are even greater.

Although much of the earlier research investigated, in a rather general sense, the relationship between social supports and coping capabilities or quality of life of elders, more recent studies have attempted to focus on the very specific conditions under which the support function provides significant benefit. Using an identity theory framework, Krause and Borawski-Clark (1994) reported that emotional support helps aged persons cope with stresses that arise in "salient social roles," those roles that are more highly valued. The value of such support in dealing with issues that emerge from personal roles that are less highly valued is not as apparent. The research has further demonstrated the means by which social support aids elderly persons. Such supportive relationships in later life benefit participants, at least in part, by restoring feelings of control and self-worth that are typically eroded under stressful circumstances. The role of self-help in restoring or augmenting elderly group members' sense of control, self-esteem, and social involvement is further confirmed under differing conditions, as well (Berkowitz, Waxman, & Yaffe, 1988).

Wellman (1981) explored social network analysis as a theoretical framework for understanding social support systems. Such an analysis allows for the complexity of interpersonal relationships rather than regarding the support system as a single, integrated structure. At the same time, it increases the possibilities of different kinds of resources as contributors to a social support system and enables the analysis of the structure of the interpersonal systems and flow of resources into those systems. Finally, it serves to connect the study of interpersonal ties to the interpretation of larger scale phenomena, relating social support to the constraints of bureaucratization and capitalism.

Numerous studies have demonstrated the benefits of social networks for older adults. The risk of isolation has been recognized as a major concern for aged people in general and even more so for older women. Greater longevity increases the risk of chronic disability and widowhood. Disability can have an impact on mobility and the opportunity for social participation. Likewise, declining social networks due to death and family mobility reduce the level of informal supports for older women. There can also be a negative impact on income when one lives a long life. Most retirees exist on fixed incomes, usually Social Security, and often pensions may be fixed. Women are harder hit by this problem because they are usually dependent on their husbands' income. When a spouse dies, household income is reduced, limiting the available resources one has to participate in social and recreational activities.

This combination of factors can greatly upset the balance between losses and gains, generating a higher degree of loss that can lead to depression and isolation among older women. Certainly, one of the major developmental tasks for olders persons is to deal with the multitude of losses that can be expected to impact on their lives. Cath (1971) referred to this as an "omniconvergence of losses" frequently including loss of income, occupation, spouse, friends and significant others, and physical functioning and mobility.

What is most essential for anyone in this situation is to promote linkage with other human beings, especially with others who are experiencing similar loss. Lowy proposed that social group work can stimulate such linkage and thereby promote more healthy aging, a view that has been promoted over time. Lang (1981) described the social work group as a unique form that operates as a mutual aid system, promoting autonomy and benefiting individual members through the effective action of the whole group. Garvin (1984) added that groups, especially those that offer support during transitional crises, can be expected to remain necessary in contemporary society, which is characterized by occupational mobility, family change, and reduced stable connections and natural support networks among people.

SUPPORT SYSTEMS AND MINORITIES

The efficacy and nature of social support systems vary greatly for subpopulations of women in later life on the basis of cultural influences and preferred patterns of support throughout earlier phases of life, among other factors. It is possible to categorize subgroups of elderly women by socioeconomic status, geography, and education, for example; however, the majority of research on the informal support function for subpopulations in the United States has focused on ethnic and racial minorities. In comparison to White women, attendance at religious functions by African American women in later life is more likely to predict informal support patterns, suggesting a pivotal role of the church in the provision of support (Hatch, 1991). There is, in addition, evidence to suggest that, in response to the stresses induced by ill health, elderly African American women are more likely than their White peers to use social supports as part of their coping strategy (Conway, 1985).

Ethnographic research has explored the relationship between cultural values and patterns of social interaction and support among aged Puerto Rican women, as well. The importance of motherhood and domestic responsibilities, and especially respect from their children and other young persons, are all driving forces in defining social support roles (Sanchez-Ayendez, 1988). Awareness of and adherence to the influences on the social support function for elderly minority women is critical in promoting, creating, or augmenting support structures.

SELF-HELP GROUPS AS SOCIAL SUPPORT

Given the preponderance of evidence highlighting the critical role of social supports and the extent to which individuals participate in social networks, it is not surprising that self-help support groups are an increasingly popular therapeutic medium. In their role as social linkage systems connecting individuals with common concerns, self-help groups are indeed sources of social support. Self-help groups may serve as substitutes for absent social networks of other sorts or may simply supplement one's existing support system. In certain situations, such as falling victim to an uncommon disorder or life circumstance, other avenues of mutual support are typically unavailable. Similarly, those who are socially isolated, by choice or circumstance, may have no alternative but to seek out a self-help group to fulfill the need for peer support.

SELF-HELP GROUPS

The term *self-help* is used in many different contexts and often has competing definitions. Self-help groups may be truly self-governing and self-regulating, or they may be led or organized by professionals, even though their goal remains that of mutual aid. Self-help groups also vary in purpose. Such groups may focus exclusively on emotional support for members, be geared primarily to social action, or provide greater functional benefits to members. Most, however, are hybrids to at least some extent.

Levy (1976) distinguished four types of self-help groups: (a) those that deal with behavior control; (b) those that address predicaments that entail some degree of stress; (c) those that are survival oriented; and (d) those that have the common goal of personal growth, self-actualization, and enhanced effectiveness in living.

All self-help groups have one common feature, that of empowerment, which helps restore or develop an all-important sense of control. For the purposes of this book, self-help is viewed in its broadest possible context and is used interchangeably with the term *mutual aid*.

History and Present-Day Demographics

During the 19th and early 20th centuries, self-help in the United States, although not known by this term, was typically provided by friendly societies, mutual benefit societies, and consumer cooperatives that assisted people with the adjustment to industrialized society. The acknowledged beginning of modern-day self-help occurred with the establishment of Alcoholics Anonymous in 1935, which spawned innumerable other 12-step programs such as Gamblers Anonymous. The growth of self-help during the 1960s and 1970s was influenced largely by the women's movement, which evolved from a focus on consciousness raising to a model that included advocacy, social, and political efforts. The gay rights movement and Mothers Against Drunk Driving, for example, subscribe to this social activism perspective. The close of the 1970s brought with it the establishment of the National Self-Help Clearinghouse and, later, many regional and local offices (Riessman & Carroll, 1995). Today, there are self-help programs for a preponderance of physical and mental health concerns, social problems, addictions, family and marital issues, oppressed populations, lifestyle alternatives, and survivor groups, as well as for a broad range of personal growth activities.

Lieberman and Snowden (1994) presented demographic data to address the question of who participates in self-help organizations. Surprisingly, men are more likely than women to use a self-help group, with a lifetime use of 3.6% as compared with one of 2.2% for women. Given the popularity of support groups for separated and divorced individuals, it is not surprising that these populations have the highest rate of participation, with lifetime use rates of 4.7% and 5.7%, respectively. When broken down by age range, persons over 60 have the lowest rate, at just 1.8%. Given the increasing prevalence and popularity of self-help programs, it is probable that future cohorts of elderly people will demonstrate higher lifetime usage rates.

The lower rates of mutual aid participation among both women of all ages and elderly men and women has implications for today's older female population. Indigenous leaders and professionals alike have a mandate to recognize gender and age cohort effects on perceptions of self-help groups and to structure programs in such a way that elderly women will be attracted to and helped by such services. In addition, psychological and physical barriers may hinder participation by those who would otherwise attend. Fear of going out alone after dark, lack of transportation, environmental challenges posed by stairs, and fear of stigmatization, among many other factors, present obstacles for older women.

An understanding of the impetus for support group participation can help guide recruitment of older women and their family and friends. Levine (1988) used the word *deviance* to describe those drawn to mutual assistance, suggesting that those who are candidates for a mutual aid group are grappling with a problem central to daily living or with a set of life circumstances that represents a departure from the norm. In other words, the individual is suffering from a problem that seems, to him or her, unique in some way. This feeling of difference and undue suffering can lead to a sense of isolation and lowered self-esteem. Levine described several factors that encourage participation in a mutual assistance organization. The individual typically views the problem or life circumstance as one that will endure over time, believes it to be socially or psychologically isolating, and has had little or no preparation or forewarning in advance of its onset.

Elements of Self-Help Groups

Although there are notable differences in the way in which support groups are structured or carried out, there are several commonalties that form the essence of this therapeutic milieu. Researchers over time have defined and reaffirmed certain essential elements (Kurtz, 1990a; Levine & Perkins, 1987; Riessman & Carroll, 1995), including the following: (a) a sense of community and affiliation through provision of a network of social relationships; (b) an ideology or paradigm that serves to convert victims to helpers; (c) the teaching of effective coping strategies for personal transformation; (d) the provision of role models for identity formation; (e) information and education; (f) an opportunity for confession, catharsis, and mutual support; and (g) advocacy and empowerment.

Foremost among the elements of mutual support groups is their capacity to generate a sense of belonging among the participants, a shared sense of suffering that creates high levels of cohesiveness (Lieberman, 1990). The shared problem reduces the sense of isolation and generates a sense of "we-ness." Because of the separation between group members (we) and those on the outside (they), the group becomes a primary support structure for the members, much like a community or family (Lieberman, 1990). At least with regard to the shared concern, members typically hold common values and acknowledge reciprocal obligations.

The support group may be conceptualized as a social microcosm in that it is a small, complete social world. Self-help groups provide a network of social relationships and a collective of interdependent individuals that value community over individualism. Members may provide concrete support to each other, such as caregiving assistance, or they may provide emotional support by sharing in successes, such as celebrating birthdays, anniversaries, and special accomplishments. Levine (1988) has noted that many members have social contact outside of the meetings. In fact, some researchers have found that members who do not develop new social relationships are less likely to improve (Lieberman, 1990).

Support group members have noted the benefits derived from helping others, not just from receiving help (Kurtz, 1990a). Levine (1988), referring to the helper-therapy principle, noted that individuals typically benefit from giving help as well as from receiving help. Other researchers have found that group members who give and receive help are more positive about the group and themselves than are members who only receive help (Maton, 1988). Several reasons for increased benefit to the helper have been postulated. First, it is easier to give than to receive help, as it increases the helper's sense of control and makes the helper feel competent and valued. In comparison, being a chronic recipient of help can be a degrading experience, eroding one's sense of self-worth. Second, by helping others, one must learn the appropriate behaviors and skills in order to teach them. This has proven to be one of the most effective means of learning. Finally, the helper receives social approval from the outside world, a benefit less likely to accrue to a recipient of aid (Riessman & Carroll, 1995). Luks (1991) coined the term *helper's high* to refer to the positive sensations experienced by those helping others. Such a high, which consists of both physical and emotional sensations, occurs immediately following the provision of help and is frequently followed by a longer phase of improved well-being. Those in Luks' study who reported experiencing this feeling—almost 95% of the study population—additionally reported better perceived health. Clearly, self-help groups create linkages that are reciprocal in nature, helping people to form relationships that provide social support that is truly mutual and beneficial.

Mutual aid groups also provide or jointly generate an ideology for the members. According to Levine (1988), every group has a unique ideology or set of beliefs about the shared problem. Antze (1976) found that each group develops a specific ideology based on the underlying psychological problem. This ideology helps members make choices by reducing uncertainty (Suler, 1984). The group develops its own language and conceptual tags for common experiences. These are used by members to interpret the experiences that are shared in the group and to assist members in processing, reprocessing, and acting on a problem. Thus ideology affects not only feelings, but choices and actions (Levine, 1988).

Personal transformation is brought about through the group's ability to blend positive and negative feedback in a supportive environment. According to Levine (1988), the sharing of distressing experiences is relieving if met with sympathetic understanding. Self-help groups offer feedback, confrontation, insight, interpretation, opportunities for goal setting, and identification with veterans who have made a successful transformation (Powell, 1987). Commonly, the group member is confronted with pressure from others to alter personal behaviors and views (Lieberman, 1990). Katz and Bender (1976) suggested that the most important aspect of support groups is their ability to reconstruct a positive identity for persons labeled as deviant.

Support groups use a variety of cognitive processes to nurture positive change. Modeling has been recognized by many researchers as an important component of support organizations (Levine, 1988; Lieberman, 1990). Hope can be found in discussions of how other members have overcome the problem, and personal transformation is achieved through deliberate or inadvertent imitation. And, as previously noted, helping peers with a common problem is a significant source of personal growth and learning for the one giving help in particular.

Self-help groups also provide a teaching function in which members receive information and education about a particular problem or affliction. Likewise, they are taught new and more successful coping mechanisms. Levy (1976) discussed the concrete suggestions group members share. This educational function includes two forms of information, that which is formally documented and that which rarely rises to that level. Levine (1988) noted that support groups provide a forum to orally transmit knowledge that does not usually get stored in any other fashion and would be lost without this exchange. Such knowledge is not, however, of lesser importance. In the case of a support group for a medical condition, for example, useful information on the daily experiences of living with or managing a disorder and its side effects typically does not appear in medical texts or patient handbooks.

Self-Help Versus Professional Help

Much attention has been paid to defining the "ideal" structure of self-help groups, particularly with regard to the leadership variable. There is considerable support for the perhaps more pure form of indigenous leadership as well as for the alternative of professionally led groups. Clinical research has confirmed the benefits of both models with regard to psychological functioning, expansion of social support networks, and improved coping skills of adult female caregivers. However, the precise nature of the improvement differs depending on leadership model. Peer-led group members displayed the greatest gains in the area of increased informal support networks, whereas members of the professionally led group exhibited the greatest improvement in psychological functioning (Toseland, Rossiter, & Labrecque, 1989). Although the study participants in Toseland et al.'s research were limited to caregivers, the results do suggest that benefits, albeit different ones, may be achieved in both peer and professionally led support groups. Given their respective functions, there is a role for both structures.

Lieberman (1990) emphasized the legitimization role that professionals can perform with support groups. Professionals can be used to identify or work with members who do not belong in the group because they need more intensive therapy, assist with the marketing function, and initiate new groups. They are equipped to share technical or medical skills with the group and the group's leader. Similarly, self-help clearinghouses, staffed by paid employees, provide a variety of services to new and established self-help groups, such as linking potential members with appropriate groups, legitimizing organizations, arranging consultation between groups, and understanding appropriate transfer of technique or ideology (Lieberman, 1990).

Lyon and Moore (1990) summarized the involvement of social workers in a group for families of murder victims by defining the professionals as active consultants in the group. Their role is more intensive during the initial phases, gradually withdrawing after the group is established. Once the group is up and running, peer group leaders are identified, and the social workers limit their direct involvement to post-meeting discussions. As the group leaders become confident in their new roles, the social workers are able to withdraw completely and remain available only on an as-needed consulting basis. In Lyon and Moore's particular case study, the group continued without direct professional facilitation and successfully increased its membership.

There are opportunities for problems to arise with both the peer and the professional leadership models, as well. Reporting on data from a survey of mental health professionals, Salzer, McFadden, and Rappaport (1994) noted that professionals involved in group leadership may actually harbor certain attitudes that may hinder collaboration with self-help organizations. Other research has shown that professionals may lack awareness of self-help groups and therefore may have less contact with them, resulting in a decreased ability to link clients who might benefit from such a group.

Many individuals choose to join support groups rather than use a formal service. Levine (1988) suggested that individuals who have chronic problems may not be adequately served by the formal service system owing to its emphasis on cure and total recovery. Costs for professional service for an extended period of time may be prohibitive, and some individuals may simply be dissatisfied with the professional service chosen. Others may be unable to satisfy certain specific needs, owing to the nature of the professional service.

Support groups are often hesitant to use professionals. Toseland and Hacker (1982) postulated various factors for this resistance, including (a) perceived loss of autonomy by members and indigenous leaders, (b) ideological conflicts, (c) apathy among professionals, (d) fear of competition for clients, and (e) skepticism by social workers and other professionals of self-help groups' effectiveness and quality.

Organizations that patently reject any professional input or participation may constrict the flow of useful information to group members and may neglect to make appropriate referrals for professional intervention. Some professionals have expressed concern regarding the ability of support groups to serve certain populations, such as vulnerable psychiatric patients. The concern is that some individuals may need more intensive, formal treatment but are steered into a self-help group that may not be able to serve their needs (Lieberman, 1990). Others have noted that the emphasis on self-help may divert resources from the formal service system, thereby reducing the amount of essential services available.

Combining the respective contributions of professionals and lay leadership to form a joint intervention can offer group participants the best of both perspectives. Collaboration by indigenous leaders and professionals, in the form of group co-leadership, has proven successful with many populations. The experience of the Elders Health Program, a Canadian treatment group for chemically dependent older adults, highlights the importance of peers as role models and sources of hope and optimism, and of professionals as facilitators of therapeutic processes (Kostyk, Fuchs, Tabisz, & Jacyk, 1993). The coleadership model may take one of two forms. Both leaders may be present and actively participate in each session, or they may take turns facilitating the group, thereby providing members a number of group sessions without an "outsider" present.

Kurtz (1990a) noted that cooperation between professionals and support groups is important for at least two reasons. First, the effective linkage of members to a group requires understanding of the group and its common concern. In addition, self-help groups can benefit from the support and credibility offered by professionals. Professional involvement can benefit self-help groups in other ways, as well. Their role may extend to include the provision of material support, such as arranging the meeting space and procuring supplies, promoting linkages between professional organizations and the self-help group, and making referrals of their clients to such support groups (Toseland & Hacker, 1982).

Kurtz (1990b) stressed that professionals should balance their involvement with support groups, suggesting that they should be neither underinvolved nor overinvolved. On the one hand, underinvolvement of professionals contributes to a lack of knowledge about support groups and decreases the likelihood of referral to groups. Overinvolvement, on the other hand, may turn the group into a bureaucratic organization that runs counter to the essence of such groups (Kurtz, 1990b). Balanced involvement by professionals may include consultation, initiation of groups, addressing the members on invitation, sponsoring groups, observing meetings, and providing technical advice.

It is important to note that individuals can benefit from use of both formal and self-help support, either simultaneously or sequentially. The experiential knowledge used by support groups may benefit a person at a certain phase in the life cycle of a problem, whereas the more objective knowledge used by the formal system may benefit the same person at another phase in their struggle (Powell, 1990). As with any therapeutic intervention, people will vary in their response to these two different approaches and must find solutions in keeping with personal preferences and beliefs.

Self-Help for Elderly Women

Despite the lower self-help group participation rates for both women and elderly people, opportunities for mutual aid for elderly women abound. Some programs such as the Supportive Older Women's Network (SOWN) cover a broad range of gender- and age-specific topics such as widowhood, menopause, financial stresses, social needs and isolation, safety issues, and health concerns (SOWN, 1992). Others have a more narrow mission.

Such self-help groups may target women of all ages, such as a mastectomy group, or may be geared to older adults regardless of gender, as in the case of Grandparents as Parents. Still others have a more narrow niche and focus exclusively on issues pertaining to older women or even on a particular problem experienced by aging or older women such as a menopause support group.

Self-Help for Friends and Family of Elderly Women

Self-help groups for friends and families coping with the negative effects of a friend's or relative's aging provide important affective and instrumental support to an often burdened population. Particularly in the case of caregivers, the need for mutual aid to battle the stresses inherent in their demanding role is significant. Self-help groups exist for spouses and adult children of those afflicted with Alzheimer's disease, friends and family of nursing home residents, relatives of hospice patients, and friends and families of patients with a large number of ailments that typically plague older adults (Kaye & Applegate, 1990a, 1990b).

Self-Help Groups for Minorities

Elderly women of ethnic and racial minorities may participate in two broad categories of self-help groups: those forged by a commonality unrelated to race or ethnicity such as widowhood and those specifically addressing an issue related to minority group affiliation, as in the case of the National Black Women's Health Project. Although there are opportunities for participation in both types of organizations, it is noteworthy that lifetime self-help group participation for all African Americans is just 1.1% as compared with 3.2% and 3.6% for Hispanics and non-minorities, respectively (Lieberman & Snowden, 1994). Even when controlling for socioeconomic status, African American lifetime usage falls well below that of non-minorities, thus eliminating the possibility that differences result from economics rather than race. Researchers have postulated a number of explanations for under-representation of African Americans in self-help organizations. First, the way in which problems are defined by the groups may be foreign to African American cultural traditions. Second, the practice of disclosing highly personal details of one's life to those who are neither family nor friends may be even more alien to African Americans than to Whites. Finally, the church and the network of church-affiliated organizations may fill, to some extent, the role held by self-help groups, thereby reducing the need for this form of intervention (Snowden & Lieberman, 1994). Snowden and Lieberman did, however, go on to point out that these explanations alone are unlikely to explain the full discrepancy between the races. Inadequate knowledge of and access to self-help groups are also probable causes. Professionals and lay persons alike have a responsibility to overcome these barriers when establishing or expanding support programs.

Investigation into self-help group participation by African Americans has suggested that mutual aid has a greater appeal when the group is relevant to their needs and readily accessible. The study of membership in a group for sickle cell disease, a disorder affecting primarily African Americans, counters the myth that this population is not attracted to groups. Rather, the results suggest that the key to participation is structuring a good fit between the needs of the population to be served and the offerings of the self-help group (Nash & Kramer, 1994).

Although the statistic for lifetime use of self-help groups by Hispanics closely approximates that of nonminorities, there is evidence to suggest that even this figure underestimates actual usage. Because of the way in which self-help is typically and, perhaps, narrowly defined, it appears that Hispanics participate less often than they do. When self-help groups are viewed as including church-affiliated groups, mutual aid organizations, and political groups, involvement by Hispanics becomes more prominent. Indeed, the self-help concept is in close harmony with Hispanic cultural philosophies of interdependence, mutual generosity, affiliation, social harmony, and collectivism (Gutierrez, Ortega, & Suarez, 1990).

Given a basic knowledge of self-help participation by minorities, what are the implications for African American and Hispanic older adults? Simply stated, the group must be tailored to the target population's needs, beliefs, and cultural norms and presented in terms indigenous to intended members. This is no more or less true for any other support group populations.

Self-Help Groups, Health Care, and the Self-Care Movement

Increasing attention to health care cost containment, changing attitudes toward doctors and the larger medical community, and an increasing emphasis on personal responsibility for health maintenance have all contributed to the modern resurgence of the self-care movement. Medical self-care—the recognition, prevention, treatment, and management of one's own health problems—has several benefits: It improves the quality of care, thereby improving health outcomes; it reduces costs through improved consumerism and decision-making skills; and it makes health care more relevant for patients—a particular concern for aged persons—by respecting their personal values (Mettler & Kemper, 1993). Social policy analysts have noted that the acceleration in the growth of self-help and mutual aid groups for the chronically ill and their families, which began in the mid-1970s, should continue as a pivotal component of health care reform (Carroll, 1994).

In gerontological circles, self-care can be seen as having a dual focus: (a) the improvement or maintenance of health as a preventive measure; and (b) as a response to the medical challenges of later life, particularly chronic illness (Mockenhaupt, 1993). It is in response to the latter function that most of the medically related self-help groups for older women have evolved. Given the common goal of personal empowerment shared by the self-care and self-help movements, it is not surprising that a self-help group exists for every major disorder recognized by the World

Health Organization (Riessman & Carroll, 1995). Support groups exist for sufferers of better known infirmities such as breast cancer, strokes, and AIDS as well as for more obscure disorders such as Hirschsprung's disease, tardive dyskinesia, and Munchausen syndrome. Health-related mutual aid organizations span both the physical and mental health categories.

Computer-Mediated Self-Help

Although many of its detractors criticize the computer for contributing to the erosion of community, lessening the need for meaningful face-to-face interaction, and making the personal impersonal, modern technology can, and does, actually play an important role in providing support. Howard Rheingold (1993) presented a compelling picture of a virtual community as just that, a community, and illustrated the numerous social, emotional, and utilitarian functions conferred to participants. Many popular on-line services such as America Online and CompuServe offer diverse support groups, including both the mutual aid and professionally mediated varieties. These groups provide unique opportunities not readily available through traditional channels, such as national and international membership, fewer physical barriers to attendance, and the automatic logging of a session's transcript. For many social problems that drive individuals to self-help groups, computer-mediated support offers the additional option of anonymity, thereby eliminating the obstacles generated by fear of stigma.

A review of a recent 3-day period of support group offerings on America Online included a broad array of forums, most of which are self-help. Groups for older adults and their families include Over Fifty & Having Fun, Widowed World, and Caregivers for Elderly Loved Ones. Other groups such as Schizophrenia Mutual Support, Depression Mutual Support, Mood Disorders Support Network, The Anxiety Annex, and Abuse Survivors' Self-Help clearly address mental health issues. Populations who might otherwise encounter physical barriers to self-help group attendance can find peer support through forums such as Multiple Sclerosis Self-Help Group, Late-Deafened Mutual Support, Cerebral Palsy Self-Help, and Post-Polio Survivors' Self-Help.

The many possibilities for technology-assisted social support, which have barely been uncovered at present, will likely burgeon as populations such as people who are homebound, people who are mobility impaired, people with agoraphobia, people with sensory impairments using computer aids, and residents of remote areas discover the benefits to be reaped. Implications for policymakers and social service professionals include the subsidization of equipment, as necessary, and the identification and training of appropriate candidates.

Consideration of computer-mediated social support for aged persons raises two cohort-specific issues: a lack of familiarity with computers and infrequent ownership of the necessary technology. Whereas today's youth will most likely own and regularly use computers for a multitude of functions as they join the ranks of the elderly, encouraging today's older generation to log on may require the use of more sophisticated technologies that are less dependent on computer skills and manual dexterity. Multimedia systems, for example, allow users to interact through voice and images rather than exclusively through keyboard inputs. Such systems are currently being used by the medical community to permit electronic home visits by nurses, for example (Kaye, 1996a). The cost of the requisite technology may be prohibitive at present, but will become more affordable as these technologies proliferate and competition among manufacturers increases.

CONCLUSION

The need for social support for all persons at every stage of life is unquestionable. And the unique role filled by self-help groups is critical to the many who choose this intervention to help cope with a variety of life circumstances. For elderly women, in particular, self-help groups can serve as a meaningful medium for support at a time when they are challenged by multiple affronts to their physical, social, familial, and economic well-being. Exactly how a self-help group for older women might function is presented in the subsequent chapters that highlight the activities of SOWN, a self-help organization designed to help women 60 years and older cope with the process of aging.

3

A Story of Empowerment:
The Case of the SOWN Program

Merle Drake and Andrea D'Asaro

In this chapter, the evolution of the SOWN program is presented from the personal perspective of those who have been involved directly in the process from the outset. Among the topics covered are the philosophy of the program, its funding and organizational history, a summary profile of its older adult participants, the defining characteristics of the SOWN group model, the use of volunteers and networking strategies, the development of replication materials, and future program directions. This chapter, by providing an overview of the various dimensions of the SOWN experience over time, serves to introduce the reader to many of the dimensions of group self-help that are then revisited, investigated, and analyzed critically in systematic fashion in the remaining chapters of the book.

THE POWER OF GROUP MEMBERSHIP

SOWN means friendships, good feelings, and airing ideas. Sharing with friends helps me grow. SOWN has enhanced my life and let me enjoy my old age.—Member of SOWN support group

Fifteen older women have gathered for their first SOWN meeting. The group facilitator asks, "What are the first words that come to your mind when you hear the phrase 'Older women are'?"

Almost instantly the participants reply, saying *wrinkled, sickly, senile, cranky,* and *useless.* There is a pause in the room as the women feel the impact of these words. They realize that these images do not accurately define them. Then, spontaneously, they begin to use words like *wise, independent, loving,* and *strong* to describe themselves. This exercise demonstrates how older women are influenced by the negative stereotypes of older women that pervade American culture.

By meeting weekly in support groups, older women across the country recognize that they are not alone. The SOWN group is a safe place to share the joys, daily realities, and sorrows of growing older. By joining together, older women learn to view old age as a series of challenges they can meet with inspiring fortitude.

WHAT DOES SOWN DO?

We share our skills and our strengths. We have found comfort in knowing we have a close-knit group of women who care, and are ready and willing to be there when needed. We are indeed SOWN together.—SOWN group member

By bringing women together, SOWN breaks down isolation and rebuilds a caring community that serves as a lifeline for group members. SOWN is one of the only agencies exclusively addressing the special needs of older women by establishing ongoing support groups in diverse locations where they live or congregate. SOWN also provides telephone reassurance, networking, counseling, community outreach, and education. SOWN groups of women over 60 years of age meet in community settings such as subsidized housing projects, churches and synagogues, apartment buildings, long-term care facilities, and senior centers.

From One Group to Hundreds

SOWN came to life with tremendous energy and very little money. A small grant enabled the first support groups to get off the ground. Drake, SOWN's founder and director, describes her inspiration for starting the Philadelphia-based agency that sprouted self-help support groups of women across the country.

At age 82, my beloved grandmother, a widow, survived only on Social Security benefits. She had lost her husband as well as two adult children while struggling with osteoporosis and arteriosclerosis. All of her family (except my mother) and friends were no longer alive. She was bombarded with losses and didn't have the supports she needed to heal and recover.

A social worker, Drake took a job at a senior center in Philadelphia to learn more about the needs of older women like her grandmother. At the center, women told her about their pain: widowhood, health concerns, poverty, crime, and loneliness. She was struck by the fact that each woman believed she was the only one struggling with these problems. To bring women together, she organized a workshop series on older women's issues.

More women came to these workshops than had ever come to the senior center. I felt the power of women helping women by the sharing of personal stories, coping strategies, tears, and laughter. At the close of the series, women didn't want the experience to end. They wanted to continue meeting in smaller groups.

Drake organized a few groups, and SOWN was born. After starting nine groups in senior centers throughout the city, Drake sought funding to launch groups in subsidized housing and long-term care facilities. Next, she offered leadership workshops for older women and professionals in the Philadelphia area. In these workshops, women were taught facilitation skills to enable them to lead their own groups. New groups were formed and a network of support grew.

Articles in local newspapers, word of mouth through the aging community, and presentations at national, regional, and local conferences spawned excitement—and new groups. Today, over a thousand women participate in the local groups; most are widowed, low income, and living alone. SOWN's staff initiates at least nine new groups each year in Philadelphia while supporting ongoing groups in the area.

Many of the very first groups formed almost 15 years ago at SOWN's inception are still meeting today as a result of the ongoing nurturing they get in the form of training and assistance. A SOWN staff member visits each group several times a year. Peer leaders call SOWN for advice on special situations such as bringing out shy members or problems with a member monopolizing the conversation. To reach out to women in the community, SOWN developed strong collaborative relationships with diverse community organizations such as the public housing authority, women's organizations, senior center networks, mental health agencies, and volunteer associations. SOWN's active governing board of directors is responsible for fiscal, planning, policy, and personnel decisions.

SOWN has begun to train volunteer leaders as part of a Volunteer Connection Program to allow groups to continue when no peer facilitator can be identified. This allows SOWN to run more groups while making the best use of its limited staff.

SOWN is also reaching out nationally as a result of hundreds of requests for guidance from organizations across the country. To respond, SOWN published a comprehensive manual and created an accompanying program of technical assistance. The package is available in the form of a membership to select organizations across the country. Membership enables agencies and individuals to purchase the manual and receive supportive training and ongoing technical assistance. A new National Support Center now assists organizations across the country who want to bring older women into nurturing SOWN groups.

SOWN'S SELF-HELP PHILOSOPHY

Throughout their lives, women crave connection and support. In the past, women shared their common experiences within churches, synagogues, and close-knit communities. Today, increased mobility and the breakdown of the extended family have severed these ties of mutual support.

SOWN's mission is to reestablish stable support networks for older women experiencing multiple losses in their lives. In the SOWN groups, women help each other cope with problems and share joys, wisdom, and pain, as well as overcome stereotypes of aging and take control of their lives. The groups become families: Members share phone calls, meals, outings, shopping, and doctors' visits and help each other through times of crisis. One SOWN member awoke from an operation to find group friends in her hospital room offering her comfort and encouraging her to come to their homes to recuperate.

SOWN knows that healing power comes from women telling their stories and receiving validation from others in similar circumstances. SOWN offers a safe place for older women to voice their strengths and touch their wisdom, compassion, and integrity. Women grow older and perhaps wiser in the context of the group's embrace.

In the group, women are empowered as the experts. They reflect on the past and solve problems in a warm circle of support. This intimacy, and the support received from SOWN, inspires 85% of groups to continue meeting.

Unlike the single-issue support groups typically formulated around specific concerns of aging (such as for families of Alzheimer's disease patients), SOWN groups address the broad spectrum of women's experience without excluding anything.

Issues women address in SOWN meetings include the following:

- self-image
- myths and realities of aging
- life review
- widowhood and grieving
- friendship
- loneliness
- housing options
- financial management
- estate planning
- health care
- assertiveness training
- volunteer options
- stress management
- family relationships
- later life careers
- social roles

The variety of issues addressed in SOWN'S informal support system buffers women against the effects of aging. Studies have found that people who have friends to turn to for advice, information, and affection are more likely to survive certain health problems. Researchers from Duke University Medical Center concluded that "a support group may be as effective as costly medical treatment. Having someone to talk to is very powerful medicine" (Brody, 1992, p. 14).

The SOWN support group model is also highly cost effective. Each group provides service to as many as 18 women. The cost per person, for each hour of contact time, is estimated to be $3.50, far less than the cost of individual therapy, for example. Another benefit of SOWN groups is the savings gained when nursing home placement is prevented or delayed by the group's nurturance and support. The closeness, disclosure of innermost feelings, and mutual concern for others keeps members coming back to their SOWN group for years and replaces isolation with community.

AGING AS A WOMEN'S ISSUE

SOWN is flourishing because women are disproportionately affected by the challenges of aging. Women make up the majority of the elderly and are more likely than men to suffer significant losses as they age. The negative images of older women in

America can undermine women's self-esteem. Fairy tales teach that older women are old bags, shrews, and scary witches. Advertising tells women that their skin should be without wrinkles and their hair without gray. Women learn that the American culture values only youthful women. In SOWN groups, women challenge this cruel picture and view themselves as powerful and creative citizens. Women re-create the supports they may have lost by outliving their network of friends and family.

SOWN knows that aging is a critical women's issue that will balloon in upcoming years. In the years ahead, SOWN hopes to have hundreds of support groups across the country working as a network to help women flourish in their old age, reverse negative stereotypes, and soften these harsh effects of aging.

FUNDING AND ORGANIZATION

SOWN agency staffing provides a model of accommodating the special needs of women. The all-female staff of part-time working women demonstrates that an organization "can allow women the freedom to raise children, work flexible hours, or pursue an education while providing a quality service," says Drake, the mother of two young children. "Awareness of the unique needs of women is a continuum that covers the whole life cycle."

SOWN started with one staff member. In 1984, the staff increased to three: the director, a direct service coordinator, and a secretary. By 1995, SOWN's staff had blossomed to seven professional social workers and counselors.

Funding sources also multiplied over the years, starting with a grant of $300 from a Philadelphia-based corporation. Over time, SOWN generated small and large private foundation support, including grants from the Pew Charitable Trust, the William Penn Foundation, and the Fannie Rippel Foundation, which supported the national expansion. In 1987, SOWN became a member agency of Women's Way, a Philadelphia-based women's fund-raising coalition. Additional backing comes from the local Area Agency on Aging, the Philadelphia Corporation on Aging, and numerous foundations and individuals.

WHO COMES TO SOWN?

Members of SOWN groups come from varying life experiences and racial, ethnic, and educational backgrounds. Despite a range of differences, the women all face similar issues of aging. SOWN groups embrace women as dissimilar as Rosalie and Bessie:

Rosalie, a 66-year-old Jewish divorcee, is a retired social worker living in Philadelphia. She once lived a middle-class lifestyle. But now her children are grown and have moved away. On a fixed income, she recently moved from her home to a studio apartment. She grieves for her old home and former life, and she can't shake her feelings of loneliness and fears that something is seriously wrong with her.

Bessie, an 85-year-old African American woman, has been widowed for 12 years. Several years ago she gave up her home to move in with her ailing sister to economize and care for her. Although fiercely proud of her ability to cope, Bessie misses her husband. She secretly believes she should not be having these feelings.

Despite their differences, Rosalie and Bessie discovered common bonds in their SOWN group as they struggled to overcome the obstacles of later life. Dissimilar members like these two often develop close relationships and grow to rely on each other like sisters and best friends.

The diverse populations in SOWN groups show that the model works for varied ethnic, economic, and racial groups. In urban Philadelphia, group members are 70% African American, 70% poor, 90% widowed and living alone, and 61% frail or handicapped. The majority of SOWN members range in age from their late 70s to early 80s. They all share the profound concerns and joys of older women.

GROUP STRUCTURE AND FACILITATION

Although every SOWN group has unique qualities, the structure is consistent with those groups started by a SOWN staff member in Philadelphia. Groups meet once a week during the day for about an hour in a community location convenient to members. Each group is composed of an average of 15 women at a given session, although membership can range from 8 to 20 women.

The SOWN model encourages women to select their own topics and ultimately assume full responsibility for facilitating the group. A professional SOWN staff member facilitates each newly formed group for approximately 20 weeks, working with the group on issues of group cohesion, confidentiality, and session plans. The SOWN facilitator moves the group toward self-sufficiency, combining a self-help approach with a respect for the members' abilities to sustain themselves. After the initial facilitation phase, the group must decide if it wants to continue and who might become the peer facilitator.

In some cases, groups require ongoing professional facilitation. For instance, a group in a nursing home may need continued professional facilitation because of the physical limitations of member residents.

In most cases, the group chooses one member from within the group to become a facilitator. Then the SOWN staff member and peer leader cofacilitate the group for the next 6–8 weeks. During this time, SOWN offers the new peer leader training followed by regular follow-up consultations. Once the peer facilitator takes over, a staff member continues to visit groups on a quarterly basis for supervision and support. In addition, all of the facilitators attend SOWN's educational seminars, which are offered several times per year.

The older women who become peer leaders are taking a risk. The Philadelphia peer facilitators leading groups today may never have assumed leader positions or received formal education in group process skills. They are breaking through personal barriers while creating a lifeline for other older women.

Like the entire SOWN network, peer facilitators come from diverse racial, ethnic, and class backgrounds. All of the peer leaders are over age 60, and many are over 80 years of age. Peer leaders say they get much more than they give as they see their lives enriched by this new and influential role.

The peer-facilitated structure allows both leaders and members to change in their outlook, often from sorrow to joy, in a safe environment, as these SOWN group members articulate:

I have learned that I have no problems that are mine alone. We older women have so very much in common. We give each other strength. I now feel younger than my 73 years. Because of SOWN I have the courage now to try new things.

Before this group I didn't remember much because of a stroke. With each meeting, I'm remembering more and more. I am recovering my memories!

It looked like my whole world was tumbling down. My husband was murdered for money to buy drugs; I lost my son-in-law to cancer. The SOWN group helped me get over a lot of things, hold on to other things, and start over again.

One SOWN group member may have summed up the feelings of many when she said, "I hope the group will be forever, so no one will be sitting around lonely without a friend, so everyone will feel wanted and loved."

THE VOLUNTEER CONNECTION

Because SOWN groups provide a rare opportunity for older women to embrace each other, new groups are requested each year in Philadelphia. To accommodate the demand for many more new groups each year, SOWN developed a new "shared" service model to increase the number of groups able to get off the ground. The Volunteer Connection, initiated in 1994, is a cadre of trained group leaders, allowing SOWN to start new groups in locations where members may not be able to run their own groups. Women with severe disabilities in long-term care facilities, for example, are not always able to make the leadership commitment because of frail health. The Connection recruits, trains, places, and oversees the network of volunteer group leaders.

Using volunteers as peer facilitators is proving effective for SOWN'S Philadelphia groups, especially in subsidized housing and residential care facilities. The Volunteer Connection, with a team of trained leaders, allows SOWN to share its expertise and expand its services.

NETWORKING

SOWN also supports networking and exchange between support groups. SOWN group members have universally requested this kind of exchange. Older women involved in a SOWN group feel a sense of power and strength in being part of a larger network of older women from all over the Philadelphia area. Individual group members receive tremendous benefit from knowing that they are not alone, that others experience their problems and want to provide support. Groups also experience confirmation and a sense of purpose in knowing that many other SOWN support groups exist to support older women and their issues. SOWN disseminates resources and information and encourages resource sharing between group leaders. SOWN also facilitates joint meetings between groups. These are powerful mechanisms for older women from diverse backgrounds to meet each other and share points of view, issues, and coping strategies. For many older women, these joint meetings are the first times in their lives when they interact closely with someone from a different racial or ethnic background.

THE POWER OF SUPPORT MANUAL

As a result of media coverage and presentations at conferences, more and more agencies across the country began to ask SOWN for advice on starting groups. In recent years, SOWN has answered over 400 requests for guidance. The shared model and a comprehensive manual and training were the beginning of SOWN's national expansion.

SOWN created the manual *The Power of Support: A Guide for Creating Self-Help Support Groups for Older Women* (Drake & Supportive Older Women's Network, 1993) to advise new groups outside Philadelphia. It is a comprehensive handbook for training social service professionals, health care practitioners, and anyone interested in developing support groups for older women in their own community. The 124-page manual, completed in 1993, explains how to start a group, become a group facilitator, and develop and lead sessions. The easy-to-use book includes session plan outlines, topics to maintain group continuity, and evaluation forms.

Developed by the SOWN staff and board, the book includes an overview of issues facing older women and guidelines on identifying meeting sites, publicizing the group, and recruiting members. Groups leaders can use topic ideas and information on group dynamics and leadership transition.

To test the effectiveness of the new manual and the accompanying training model, SOWN piloted the program at 18 new groups run by Philadelphia agencies. Each agency received a manual, basic training for the staff or volunteer leader, and extensive technical assistance and consultation. SOWN found that such ongoing training, support, technical assistance, and follow-up is essential to supplement the manual.

SOWN now offers the manual as a benefit of national membership along with intensive training and technical assistance to help organizations start and maintain their own groups.

CONCLUSION:
THE NATIONAL SUPPORT CENTER AND THE FUTURE

Words of praise for the manual in aging and professional publications brought in requests for membership from across the country to the Philadelphia office. Since the national program began, SOWN has formed membership relationships with agencies and organizations all over the United States and in Canada, now running SOWN groups. One program in Tennessee started nine support groups for older women using SOWN's shared model.

To provide training and assistance to new member organizations, a National Support Center was added to SOWN's local branch in 1993 as the foundation of the shared national model. New national SOWN members have reported that the manual and accompanying program are practical and comprehensive. Looking to the future, SOWN is working to expand the national membership program to encourage and support more groups where they are needed.

In keeping with the age of technology, SOWN has developed new ways to bring groups of women together, such as via the Internet and telephone conference calls. These "virtual groups" will reach homebound women who cannot travel to a central location. SOWN groups will continue to evolve, bringing older women together to overcome the problems of loneliness and loss. SOWN enables other women to discover their own resources of power and resilience.

4

Characteristics of Older Women and Peer Facilitators in Self-Help Groups

This chapter as well as chapters 5–7 present the results of in-person interviews conducted with older women and their support group facilitators in the greater Philadelphia metropolitan area. This information is supplemented by interviews performed with the program staff of Philadelphia's SOWN. These sources of information add qualitative detail and richness to the statistical analysis of survey questionnaires completed by group members and facilitators associated with the SOWN program reported on in these same chapters. As a result, chapters 4–7 should provide a comprehensive picture of the SOWN experience for older female participants, those who have assumed responsibility for peer facilitating these mutual support groups, and professionals who staff the program. These chapters aim to provide an empirical backdrop against which the personal "painting" of the historical evolution of the SOWN program as presented in the preceding chapter can be appreciated and interpreted. These chapters should also provide the reader with considerable direction in terms of what is required to make support groups successful vehicles for promoting the self-help efforts of older women.

Before presenting findings from the local survey, a brief review of the investigative procedures and methods adhered to in conducting the research is offered. Additional details concerning statistical procedures can be found in appendix A.

HOW THE RESEARCH WAS PERFORMED

This book reports the results of a project that collected a variety of information from persons in the Philadelphia metropolitan area involved with a series of self-help support groups under the auspices of SOWN. Information was also collected elsewhere in the United States from a select group of programs providing similar kinds of self-help group services for older women. The methods adhered to in collecting the information from the Philadelphia metropolitan area SOWN are described in this section. Chapter 8 includes a summary of the methods that were followed in identifying self-help group experts and collecting data from alternative self-help group programs elsewhere in the United States.

THE APPROACH TO COLLECTING INFORMATION
IN THE PHILADELPHIA AREA

Areas of Investigation

The central research issues and the specific variables measured during the Philadelphia metropolitan area phase of the project are outlined here.

KEY VARIABLES STUDIED IN THE FIVE MAJOR AREAS
OF RESEARCH INQUIRY

AREA 1: The Characteristics of Older Women Engaged in Self-Help Groups
- Age
- Marital status
- Number and location of children
- Living arrangements
- Race or ethnicity
- Education
- Employment status
- Volunteer status
- Income status
- Health status and problems

AREA 2: The Characteristics of Self-Help Peer Group Facilitators
- Study variables listed in Area 1, above
- Frequency of group facilitation
- Length of service as facilitator
- Previous experience with self-help groups
- Stressful aspects of group facilitation
- Most or least satisfying aspects of group facilitation
- Problem areas for group facilitators
- Effectiveness of group facilitators
- Reasons for becoming a group facilitator
- Process of becoming a group facilitator
- Areas of needed training

AREA 3: The Structure of Self-Help Group Programs
- Public or private status
- Profit or nonprofit status
- Sectarian or nonsectarian auspice
- Sources of funding
- Geographic boundaries of service provision
- Program goals and objectives
- Type and range of services provided
- Support groups
- Leadership seminars
- Consultative and outreach services
- Newsletters
- Networking
- Size of the groups
- Eligibility criteria for participation
- Location of groups
  - Senior and community centers

- Apartment buildings and housing projects
- Churches and synagogues
- Long-term care facilities

AREA 4: The Functioning of Self-Help Group Programs
- Techniques for developing peer leadership skills
- Techniques for marketing self-help programs for older women
- Self-help group topics or subjects covered
- Techniques for building group cohesiveness
- Techniques for dealing with dysfunctional group dynamics
- Techniques for evaluating program effectiveness and impact

AREA 5: The Impact of Self-Help Groups
- Measures of self-help program success
- Extent to which caring support systems are reestablished
- Extent to which mutual support is increased
- Extent to which anxiety about aging problems is reduced
- Extent to which isolation and sense of impotence is reduced
- Extent to which knowledge of coping resources is increased in times of crisis
- Degree of comfort in sharing experiences
- Level of participation in self-help program
- Level of participant satisfaction and dissatisfaction
- Most effective and least effective self-help program strategies
- Adequacy of resources (funds, staff, time)
- Major shortcomings of current self-help initiatives
- Future initiatives planned in older adult self-help

The research team was especially interested in collecting information in five major areas: (a) characteristics of the participating older women, (b) characteristics of the peer group facilitators, (c) the structure of group programs, (d) the functioning of group programs, and (e) the efficacy of group programs.

Information Sources and Sampling Strategy

During the Philadelphia area phase of the research, information was collected from three groups of people: (a) two hundred twenty-five older women participating in 24 self-help groups in Pennsylvania's Greater Delaware Valley, operated by SOWN, (b) 14 support group facilitators carrying responsibility for groups currently operating as part of SOWN, and (c) SOWN staff.

As described in Chapter 3, SOWN is a unique nonprofit agency dedicated to helping older women (60 years and older) living in the Philadelphia area cope with specific aging problems. The majority of older people entering SOWN's services have experienced multiple losses (e.g., widowhood, loss of friends and relatives, and loss of physical health and mobility).

SOWN's services were developed on the basis of a self-help delivery model. The primary services provided by SOWN are ongoing support groups for older women, leadership seminars that train older women to be group facilitators, consultative and outreach services, a newsletter, and networking. The core service of this agency is the establishment of support groups in different community locations. The mobile, on-the-road premise of the program speaks to the importance of bringing programming to where it is needed and can be conveniently used by older women (Greene, 1992). Since its inception in 1982, SOWN has initiated dozens of groups and served many hundreds of older women in various locations throughout the greater Philadelphia area. On an annual basis, approximately 85% of the groups choose to continue meeting as an ongoing service for their members.

ANTECEDENTS OF THE PROJECT

Two structured research questionnaires were used in this research. The first was designed to gauge the experiences of older women as SOWN group members. The second was designed to assess the experiences of SOWN group facilitators. The group member questionnaire contained 33 forced-choice or open-ended questions. The group facilitator questionnaire contained 37 items. These instruments served to operationalize a large proportion of the list of study variables presented above under Areas of Investigation.

The study instruments were field-tested during the course of their development. Group administration of the questionnaires with SOWN group participants commenced in 1990 and continued over approximately a 2-year period. Questionnaire data were eventually collected from 24 groups, or 225 group members and 14 group facilitators.

During the period in which questionnaires were administered to SOWN groups, the number of members and facilitators in groups and the number of groups themselves necessarily varied. It is therefore difficult to determine a precise response rate in terms of those who participated in this phase of the project. Thus, the response rates presented are based on SOWN participant data at a single point in time. SOWN staff reported that at the completion of questionnaire administration the organization included 373 group members and 33 facilitators who comprised 32 active SOWN groups. On the basis of those membership statistics, response rates for questionnaire data are 60.3% and 42.4% for SOWN members and facilitators, respectively. These questionnaire responses represent a substantial quantitative database for the analysis and represent persons who have been involved in SOWN groups for varying periods of time, ranging from 6 months to 8.5 years.

THE QUALITATIVE INTERVIEWS

In addition to structured questionnaire data, in-depth interview data were derived from a series of intensive field interviews conducted with randomly selected group members, facilitators, and program staff subsequent to the completion of the survey questionnaires. The findings from this phase of the project are interspersed throughout this chapter and chapters 5–7.

A total of 94 members and 12 facilitators were originally chosen to be interviewed, with 50 members and 10 facilitators agreeing ultimately to participate in the interview process. Interviews were conducted with the following SOWN program personnel as well: the executive director, managing director, direct service coordinator, and group facilitator. Of the 10 facilitators interviewed, 3 were SOWN staff (two social workers and one a former peer facilitator who works part time at one of the SOWN meeting sites). The two social workers are not included in the personal profiles of group facilitators presented later in this chapter.

Field interviewers of group members and facilitators used two semistructured, open-ended questionnaires. These instruments were similar, with the exception of more detailed questions prepared for the facilitators in terms of leadership skills, training, and challenges in running the group. The questionnaires also tapped selected study variables specified in the text box *Key Variables Studies in the Five Major Areas of Research Inquiry,* but from a qualitative perspective. Intensive in-person field interviews were conducted with SOWN staff by means of a semistructured, 19-question research interview guide that focused on tapping the techniques, methods, and processes of mounting self-help group programs for older women. Additional data on self-help programming, older women, and the SOWN experience are incorporated in this analysis, including information culled from interviews with SOWN staff, students, experts, and other key informants completed in 1995 and 1996.

All respondents participating in field interviews were advised of the voluntary nature of the study and that their responses would be treated with full confidentiality. Older women were interviewed either at home or at the SOWN meeting site, whenever the latter was possible. In general, participants in the project proved quite responsive to and appreciative of being chosen to be interviewed.

Taken together, the analyses reported in subsequent chapters weigh the relative contributions of varying individuals associated with the SOWN self-help delivery model. It takes into account perspectives of both consumers (participating older women and their group facilitators) and providers (self-help group experts and study site staff) of the service.

Dominant methods and techniques of self-help group development recommended by the national sample of self-help group program experts (chapter 8) and used by the case-study self-help group site program (SOWN) were integrated in constructing a series of "best practice" guidelines for mounting a self-help delivery model in other regions of the country (see chapters 8 and 10).

As seen later in this chapter, the personal characteristics of the women who participate in self-help groups are quite varied in terms of socioeconomic background, geographic location, financial circumstances, and health or physical condition. However, many of their responses regarding how self-help groups have changed or in some way affected their individual lives center around the same undeniable themes. The common threads of closeness, of feeling as though the group was like a family, of disclosing one's innermost feelings for perhaps the first time, and of the mutual concern for one another are all sentiments that are virtually universal in the stories told by the older women who participate in these groups, the older women who peer facilitate the groups, and the professionals who staff the programs.

WHAT WAS LEARNED

In this chapter, findings are presented that describe the demographic characteristics of SOWN group members and facilitators, as compiled from questionnaire data and personal interviews. Subsections include the following: a demographic profile of

SOWN group members, demographic characteristics of members by race and marital status, living companions of group members, parenting characteristics of group members, participation patterns in other support groups by SOWN members, major life and health changes experienced in the past year by group members, emotional changes experienced in the past year by SOWN group members, and a demographic profile of SOWN group facilitators. Tables are included where appropriate to organize statistics.

A DEMOGRAPHIC PROFILE OF SOWN GROUP MEMBERS

In this section, basic demographic characteristics of the older female group members are presented, including their age, marital status, race, education, employment status, health status, and specific health problems they are likely to be experiencing (see Table 4-1). These data build on the introductory profile of group members presented in chapter 3. With respect to age, approximately half of all SOWN members are between 70 and 79 years old. An additional 30% are in their 80s, and slightly more than 15% of members are in their 60s. Fewer than 5% of group members are younger than 60 years old or more than 90 years of age. The average age of a group participant is 76.1 years.

As might be expected, the majority of SOWN group members are widowed (71.7%), and the remaining 28.3% are married, divorced, separated, or single. Clearly, then, SOWN participation is not commonly an activity that women who are married and living with their spouses are likely to engage in. Less than 2 in every 10 group participants (14.6%) are married.

With respect to race, most members are either White (72.9%) or African American (25.6%), with only 3 group members representing other racial identities (Native American and Asian American).

The average number of years of education attained by group members is 10.9. Approximately 11% of the respondents had an eighth-grade education or less, and about 50% were high school graduates.

The majority of group members were retired (68.9%), and about 17% stated that they were unemployed; another 11% defined themselves as homemakers. Fewer than 3% of SOWN group members stated that they were currently employed.

With respect to self-reported health status, approximately 86% of group members stated that their health was good or fair. About 10% reported that they were in excellent health, and fewer than 5% defined their current health as poor. The most commonly reported specific health problems were arthritis and high blood pressure (reported by 33.3% and 25% of the women, respectively), with heart problems and diabetes the next most prevalent conditions. Fewer than 2% of group members specified that they suffered from cancer. Thus, SOWN participants were, not uncommonly, confronted with one or more chronic health conditions that contributed to their health status being granted a rating that was less than excellent but better than poor.

As discussed in chapter 3, for those groups operating directly in urban Philadelphia, the majority of participants are widowed, low-income African Americans living alone and confronted with disabling conditions. It many respects, such a profile may be said to be signaling the increased attractiveness of self-help programming to those who have traditionally been its most sparse if not hesitant consumers—at-risk women of color.

Table 4-1 A statistical portrait of older women participating in SOWN support groups

Variable	Frequency	%
Age		
<60 years	2	1.1
60–69 years	31	16.3
70–79 years	96	50.5
80–89 years	56	29.5
>90 years	5	2.6
Marital status		
Widowed	142	71.7
Married, living with spouse	29	14.6
Divorced or separated	17	8.6
Never married	10	5.1
Race		
White	148	72.9
African American	52	25.6
Native American	2	1.0
Asian American	1	0.5
Education		
8th grade or less	19	11.1
Some high school	47	27.5
High school graduate	82	47.9
More than high school	23	13.5
Employment status		
Retired	126	68.9
Unemployed	32	17.5
Homemaker	20	10.9
Employed part time	4	2.2
Employed full time	1	0.5
Health status		
Excellent	20	9.5
Good	90	43.1
Fair	90	43.1
Poor	9	4.3
Specific health problems		
Arthritis	112	33.3
High blood pressure	84	25.0
Heart problems	52	15.5
Diabetes	36	10.7
Stroke	13	3.9
Mental health	6	1.8
Cancer	5	1.5
Other	28	8.3

Note. SOWN = Supportive Older Women's Network.

Demographic Characteristics by Race and Marital Status

In this section, several demographic factors are considered along racial and marital status lines, including age, education, volunteer status, income, and health status. Whites and African Americans are considered in this analysis as the sizes of these groups were large enough for the comparisons to be meaningful. It can be concluded that White group members were significantly older (by approximately 4 years; 77 years as compared with 72.9 years, respectively), had an average of 1.3 more years of education (11.2 years as compared with 9.9 years, respectively), and were less likely to volunteer their services and more likely to have higher incomes. However, Whites and African Americans were roughly equal with respect to self-reported health status.

Comparisons were also made between those group members currently married and those presently widowed, separated, or divorced along the same demographics specified immediately above. Currently married group members were, on average, significantly younger (72.9 years as compared with 76.6 years) and significantly more educated (11.8 years compared with 10.6 years). They did not differ significantly from those who are widowed, separated, or divorced in terms of income level and health status. Group members from both marital status categories were also equally likely to engage in volunteer activities.

Living Companions of SOWN Members

In the questionnaire, members were asked to report with whom, if anyone, they lived. This information can to some extent be used to evaluate the degree of support these women had in their lives. The majority of SOWN group members lived alone (57.1%). Much smaller percentages lived with a husband (14.3%) or with a child or grandchild (13%). The remaining members reported that they lived with friends, parents, in-laws, siblings, or other relatives.

Parenting Characteristics of SOWN Members

Approximately 85% of SOWN members had one or more children. Of those who did, approximately 23% reported that their children lived in close proximity to them, and almost 13% stated that they lived, geographically speaking, far away. Approximately 23% of the women noted that their children were helpful to them, and fewer than 4% described their children as unhelpful. Almost 18% of respondents reported that they saw their children regularly, and about 12% noted infrequent contact. Twenty-nine group members (7.8%) had been predeceased by one or more children.

SOWN Member Participation in Other Support Groups

The older women who were engaged in SOWN activities were not veteran support group participants. For approximately 70% of group members, SOWN was the first support group with which they had been involved. Of the remaining 30% who had been or were currently involved in other support groups, 49 members had been involved in one or two other support groups (87.5%), whereas 7 members had been involved with three or more other support groups (12.5%). An extended discussion of these women's experiences in other categories of groups and associations is presented in chapter 6.

Major Life Changes and Health Changes Experienced in the Past Year by SOWN Members

In this section, data are reported in which group members described the types of major life and health changes that they have experienced during the previous year. Some respondents described more than one major life or health change. The most commonly reported major life change involves becoming widowed (see Table 4-2), which 31 SOWN members had experienced in the past year (13.8%). Although an additional 19 members (8.5%) noted a decrease in income, it is interesting to note that 13 (5.8%) reported an increase in income (highlighting the fact that major life changes need not be negative in all cases). Other major life changes less frequently described included moving from one's home, having a child move away, having a child die, and getting married, divorced, or separated.

With respect to health changes, group members responded to questions that inquired into the levels and types of health changes they had experienced. Once again, it was discovered that such health changes need not reflect, necessarily, decline or deterioration in one's personal health. Most respondents (89) reported that they had experienced no change in their health (42.8%). However, about 35% of group members reported that their health had improved either by a lot (48) or a little (24). A total of 47 group members noted that their health had declined to some extent (22.6%).

Of those who specified what type of health change they had experienced, 53.2% reported a negative physical health change, and 17.7% noted a positive physical health change. Of those experiencing mental health changes, 24.1% (19) reported a

Table 4-2 Major life changes experienced in the past year by support group members

	Yes		No	
Change	N	%	N	%
Became widowed	31	13.8	193	86.2
Income decreased	19	8.5	205	91.5
Income increased	13	5.8	211	94.2
Moved to retirement community	10	4.5	214	95.5
Moved to senior housing	10	4.5	214	95.5
Child moved far away	8	3.6	216	96.4
Lost child through death	5	2.2	219	97.8
Married	5	2.2	219	97.8
Divorced or separated	4	1.8	220	98.2
Moved out of own home	4	1.8	220	98.2
Moved to children's home	3	1.3	221	98.7
Moved to nursing home	1	0.4	223	99.6
Other	12	5.4	212	94.6

positive mental health change in the past year; only 1 respondent (1.2%) stated that she had experienced a negative mental health change.

Emotional Changes Experienced in the Past Year

In this section, group members' descriptions of the types of mental and emotional health changes they have experienced in the past year are reported in greater detail. In the questionnaire, respondents were asked to indicate, from a checklist, all of the emotional changes that they had experienced during the previous year (see Table 4-3). The most commonly reported emotional change was "feel more connected to others," which was experienced by slightly more than half of all respondents (51.1%, or 115). Another 96 group members noted that they felt more interested in life (42.7%), and 85 stated that they felt happier (37.8%). It is interesting to see that the women were more likely to acknowledge positive changes having occurred in the past 12 months than they were to acknowledge negative ones. Thus, the women less commonly cited emotional changes that might be characterized as undesirable such as feeling sadder (14.7%) or feeling an increased sense of loss (7.1%) and a decreased sense of self-worth (7.1%). Only 7 group members noted that they had felt less connected to others over the past year (3.1%). Of course, the reader should remember that these changes in the emotional health status of the women, whether positive or negative, cannot necessarily be attributed at this point to support group participation.

Profiles of Group Members and Facilitators
Participating in Face-to-Face Interviews

The largest proportion of group members who were interviewed personally (50%) fell into the 70–79-year-old category. Thirty-seven (74%) of those interviewed were widows. Almost 30% of those interviewed had achieved a college or graduate school

Table 4-3 Emotional changes experienced in the past year

	Yes		No	
Emotional change	N	%	N	%
Feel more connected to others	115	51.1	110	48.9
Feel more interested in life	96	42.7	129	57.3
Feel happier	85	37.8	140	62.2
Feel more cared for	83	36.9	142	63.1
Feel increased sense of self-worth	67	29.8	158	70.2
Feel decreased sense of loss	39	17.3	186	82.7
Feel sadder	33	14.7	192	85.3
Feel increased sense of loss	16	7.1	209	92.9
Feel decreased sense of self-worth	16	7.1	209	92.9
Feel less interested in life	14	6.2	211	93.8
Feel less cared for	10	4.4	215	95.6
Feel less connected to others	7	3.1	218	96.9
Other	4	1.8	221	98.2

degree, and 33% possessed a high school diploma, including 9% with additional postgraduate training, either in business or nursing. These women were most likely to be residing in private residences, with 72% of the group members still maintaining either their own apartment or house. Thus, those older women who were interviewed reflected a demographic profile that is exceedingly similar to those whose participation was limited to the completion of the questionnaire.

A DEMOGRAPHIC PROFILE OF SOWN GROUP FACILITATORS

In this section, the same demographic characteristics considered for group members are used to describe the 14 group facilitators who responded to the facilitator questionnaire (see Table 4-4). Their profiles, as compared with those of group participants, reflect a somewhat younger, healthier, more educated group of women

Table 4-4 A statistical portrait of facilitators of SOWN support groups

Variable	Frequency	%
Age		
<40 years	3	23.1
40–60 years	3	23.1
>60 years	7	53.8
Marital status		
Widowed	6	46.2
Married, living with spouse	5	38.6
Divorced or separated	1	7.6
Never married	1	7.6
Race		
White	10	71.4
African American	3	21.4
Other	1	7.2
Education		
≤12 years	3	21.4
>12 years	11	78.6
Employment status		
Employed full time	6	42.8
Retired	4	28.6
Employed part time	2	14.3
Homemaker	2	14.3
Health status		
Excellent	6	42.9
Good	7	50.0
Fair	1	7.1
Specific health problems		
Arthritis	3	30.0
High blood pressure	2	20.0
Heart problems	1	10.0
Cancer	1	10.0
Other	3	30.0

who were more likely to be employed and married. More than half of these women were over 60 years of age (53.8%), whereas the remaining 6 facilitators were younger than 60. With respect to marital status, 6 facilitators were widowed (46.2%), 5 were married (38.6%), and 1 was divorced (7.6%). Most facilitators were White (71.4%), 3 were African American (21.4%), and 1 was identified as a member of an unspecified racial category. Facilitators were all high school graduates, and 78.6% of them had some schooling beyond high school. Group facilitators were more likely than members to be employed (57.1%) and less likely to be retired (28.6%) or homemakers (14.3%). With respect to health status, the majority of facilitators responded that their health was good or excellent (92.9%), with only 1 facilitator describing her health as fair (7.1%). Specific health problems mentioned included arthritis (3), high blood pressure (2), heart problems (1), and cancer (1).

CONCLUSION

As the research findings indicate, the self-help group participants vary with regard to socioeconomic factors, financial status, and health, among other characteristics. However, as will be addressed subsequently, such differences do not necessarily impede the successful establishment and ongoing operations of women's support groups. In many cases, the presence of members with different life experiences and viewpoints enhances the therapeutic function while in others the number and/or importance of commonalities outweighs the differences. Indeed, as shall be seen, there appear to be many nearly universal experiences for the population of older women described herein.

Having described the methods by which data were collected during the course of the research and profiled self-help support group participants and peer facilitators from a comprehensive sociodemographic perspective, it is time to proceed to an analysis of the SOWN support group process itself. How are SOWN groups organized? What features predominate the SOWN group meeting? Do SOWN groups really make a difference in older women's lives? These questions and many others are answered in the next three chapters.

5

The Organization of Self-Help Group Programs

In this chapter, a detailed description of the organizational characteristics of self-help delivery group programs as conceived by SOWN are presented. The perspectives of group participants, group facilitators, and program staff are included in constructing this detailed structural profile of a model self-help support group program for older women. Considered here are strategies for starting up and maintaining the groups; training processes; specific features of the groups that are considered to be more and less successful; member participation patterns; recommended group discussion topics; the roles of group members, group facilitators, and professional staff; and a description of a typical group meeting. Material presented here as well as in chapter 6 builds substantially on the initial profiling of the major elements or dimensions of the SOWN program described by Drake and D'Asaro in chapter 3.

ORGANIZATIONAL PROFILE OF SOWN

Administrative and direct service staff were interviewed during this stage of the research. The executive director, the originator of the SOWN concept, had been with the program since its beginnings approximately 12 years ago. The other women had been employed by the program for periods ranging from 6 months to 14 months. The executive director, who works 25–30 hours a week, is responsible for fund-raising, staffing the board, supervising the direct service staff, and budgeting. The managing director, who works 12–15 hours a week, is responsible for special projects, editing the newsletter, developing marketing materials, serving on the board of one of the funding sources (Women's Way), and handling other selected administrative tasks. The direct services coordinator oversees the group facilitators, does outreach to start new groups, facilitates new groups, provides technical assistance to ongoing groups, trains group facilitators, and develops materials for group sessions. Finally, the group facilitators monitor the progress of the groups over time, deal with issues that arise from the groups, participate in training sessions, assist in starting new groups, and visit the groups periodically.

The SOWN program uses volunteers on a regular basis. Volunteers are used, in particular, to facilitate separate SOWN groups. Additional volunteer facilitators join

SOWN periodically depending on the number of groups that are starting up and in need of facilitation assistance. Board members, older adults, and local college and university students placed with the program as part of field practica contribute as volunteers on a regular basis as well. The volunteer component of the program appears to be growing in importance and represents a critical resource for staff given the difficulties of securing external funding that is earmarked to enhance the size of the agency's personnel pool. Voluntarism appears also to mesh well in programs such as these with the concept of self-help. SOWN's Volunteer Connection, established in 1994 and described in chapter 3, has served to formalize the organization's commitment to volunteer service.

As described in chapter 3, SOWN has secured support for its efforts from a variety of funding sources. Even so, one of the current challenges for programs of this type is discovering government funding opportunities. City and state funding has been received by SOWN in the past but has more recently been cut back. SOWN has traditionally realized greatest success when appealing to private foundations, not-for-profit community funding groups, and corporate funding bodies. Such monies have served to stabilize the SOWN budget (annual budgets averaged $65,000–$70,000 annually before 1987 and have more recently averaged $130,000–$150,000 or more a year).

Program personnel interviewed were asked to describe those aspects of the organization that work most effectively and efficiently for SOWN. Positive features cited include the small staff, which had been stable for extended periods of time. It is important to keep in mind that the staff work with very clear job descriptions yet are sensitive to the need to be flexible in terms of role performance. Staff also appear to function in an atmosphere that is cooperative and well integrated and that provides consistent supervision, especially in terms of dealing with a variety of clinical issues faced by the participating older women. Programs in older adult self-help can expect to deal with a range of personal issues confronted by women as they experience the challenges of aging.

Another strength of the program cited by staff is the organization's steadfast focus on empowering women. Empowerment as a focal point has apparently come to be a trademark or identifying marker for the SOWN project. Such a feature is highlighted during the course of marketing the groups and recruiting other older women as new group members. It clearly differentiates the SOWN program from most other community projects serving elderly people generally and older women in particular. The concept of empowerment also seems to mesh well with the philosophy of self-help. Effort is constantly being made to tap the experience and natural expertise of the women participating in SOWN.

Challenges cited in the organizational structure of SOWN are likely not to be that much different from similar such programs operating elsewhere in the country. First is the challenge to serve as many women as the program would like to. The need for self-help services is believed to be great, but available resources inevitably limit the scope and breadth of programmatic efforts. There is a sense that programs of self-help support may need to be particularly sophisticated marketers who can educate the larger community about the benefits of self-help. It would seem that many funding sources (including both the public and private sectors) are not particularly knowledgeable about self-help and may perceive it to be less concrete or tangible a service entity as compared with many other elder program services such as congregate meals programs, special housing, recreation programs, and adult day care. It is believed that fewer than 1% of the population who could benefit from the program currently make use of it. Similarly, limited and extremely mobile staff create some challenges in maintaining effective lines of communication and accomplishing certain time-consuming tasks such as preparation of the newsletter *SOWN's Sounding Board.*

A second challenge is associated with communicating adequately within the particular neighborhood or facility in which a SOWN group is operating. Considerable time and effort is required to turn the community on to SOWN's message of women's empowerment. Many older women, especially those who have subscribed for much of their lives to traditional notions of women's role and function in society, are not all that well informed on issues of self-help and mutual aid. The concept of personal empowerment and advocacy is, not uncommonly, quite foreign to these women's view of life and problem solving.

A third challenge has to do with finding the time necessary to collaborate adequately with other community agencies' programs. Given the limited size of staff attached to programs of this type, personnel, as a rule, can be expected to carry multiple and extensive responsibilities. The demands associated with maintaining basic program operations inevitably deplete the available reservoir of time and energy remaining available for supplementary organizational functions such as attending interagency councils, sitting on community boards and advisory groups, and collaborating with other organizations engaged in service to the older adult community.

A fourth challenge may be characterized as the inevitable risk that staff and facilitator vision could come to reflect undue reliance on conventional or traditional methods in terms of how to handle particular issues and problems that arise during group meetings. This is not to say that there are no tried-and-true strategies for dealing with dysfunctional group dynamics—there are, and these techniques should not be abandoned. However, the knowledge base in older adult group functioning is regularly being updated, refined, and expanded. Staff and facilitators take seriously the responsibility to remain well informed about such developments and innovation in group problem solving. Having more than one group facilitator share responsibilities for a particular group may help to guard against any unwillingness to consider new and innovative approaches to problem resolution.

A fifth and final challenge has to do with the capacity to let groups go should circumstances warrant it. Organizing and establishing stable groups is a demanding task. Inevitably, there are likely to be significant measures of both intellectual and emotional commitment associated with the process. The decision to terminate or shut down a group can be exceedingly difficult. The challenge for staff, facilitators, and group members lies in their ability to analyze objectively the status of the group in terms of whether it has accomplished its goals and objectives or whether it is continuing to function at a level that is adequate enough to justify its continued operation.

Long range goals of SOWN include the following:

- ongoing expansion of a comprehensive replication manual and training video so that the concept of SOWN can continue to be developed in other communities;

the replication manual has already been developed and undergoes periodic revisions and updates so that the material remains current

- providing technical assistance to other communities wishing to use SOWN techniques; this appears to be an increasingly important element of the enterprise as reflected in the work of the SOWN National Support Center established in 1993 and described earlier in chapter 3
- developing a proprietary arm of the organization through which individual, family, and group therapy could be offered as opposed to assistance solely with developing successful support groups for older women
- establishing a "service maintenance" emphasis within the program such that more thorough follow-up can be provided to ongoing SOWN groups
- establishing new support groups for older women having special needs

As reported in chapter 3 and noted above, SOWN is already realizing its longer range goals in many respects. Recently, it has begun developing specialized session materials for a variety of categories of self-help groups composed of older women with dementia, hearing deficits, blindness, and low vision needs and even of retired nuns. SOWN has also recently organized a group for severely disabled older women who are virtually homebound. The group convenes by means of conference telephone technology every Friday morning. Included among the five African American older women who make up the group is a woman crippled severely by arthritis, one who is blind, and one who is a double amputee. The women in this group are already contacting each other by telephone between meetings and establishing what may well be long-term relationships.

SOWN staff were also queried as to what programs would be implemented if the program had unlimited funds available to them. High on the wish list are these:

- a clinical component able to offer counseling services
- a stronger advocacy or legislative arm (similar to that of the Older Women's League) that could press for policy change in the areas of long-term care insurance, Social Security, and related economic matters. Included here is the desire to serve as a clearinghouse for resources, referrals, and assistance with grants-seeking efforts
- travel funds to enable more aggressive replication efforts by staff in other communities
- a transportation program to assist women in more easily attending SOWN group meetings
- implementation of a major oral history project and development of a documentary film and book describing the evolution of SOWN
- specialized housing for older women that would represent a supportive shared housing community

STARTING UP AND MAINTAINING SOWN GROUPS

The SOWN program uses a variety of marketing strategies in reaching out to the older adult community, including press releases, appearances on radio and television talk shows, public service messages on television, flyers, use of the agency's board, speaking at conferences, and participating in community health fairs.

The process involved in starting up a new group entails outreach into the prospective site, whether it be a senior center, older adult housing residence, or local community center. An outreach meeting, which is primarily informational, is held at a convenient site to explain what SOWN groups are about and to build up interest in the SOWN idea. Flyers are also posted around the prospective location, especially if prospective group members are not situated in a particular building. Approximately 3 weeks later, the group is chosen. Ground rules for being a member are mutually established at the first meeting subsequent to the outreach meeting.

The obligations accompanying the acceptance of earmarked funding have come, in large part, to determine when and where new groups are organized. For example, a funding source may require that its support be used for organizing groups in long-term care facilities or public housing residences. This was not the case earlier on in the life of SOWN when sources of financial support were less likely to be earmarked for particular activities. As a result, prospective sites may find themselves put on a waiting list until specialized financial support can be obtained to meet the costs associated with group planning and operation in that particular locale.

As was discussed in chapter 3, once established, groups are closely monitored for approximately 20 weeks and as many as 25 or 30. This entails the actual facilitation of the group by a staff person leading up to transition (whenever possible) from staff to peer leadership. During this time, staff are observing and beginning to identify possible peer facilitators and promoting their transformation from group members to group facilitators. Subsequent to the initial 20- to 30-week monitoring period, follow-up monitoring by program staff is performed approximately three times annually.

SOWN staff have definite opinions as to those factors that make a strong group and the reasons why a group might disband. A strong group is characterized by members having a powerful sense of the group and high valuation for personal sharing. Some degree of optimism and a sense that problems are not intractable are important as well. Sessions progress well when the staff's and facilitators' sense of reality meshes reasonably well with the group members' sense of reality. Finally, groups progress even further when they are able to cut through extraneous matters and are willing to address the issues at hand.

In some cases, it is determined that it is better for a group to disband. Reasons leading to the decision to disband include the following:

1. The group may realize that it has accomplished its objectives or outlived its purpose. At that time, members may break into smaller more informal groups or discontinue meeting altogether.
2. The facilitator may become burned out or sick or be pulled away for some other reason, and there is no available person to substitute as facilitator. The ability to rotate leadership often seems to make for a stronger, more flexible group that can better withstand unanticipated withdrawal by a particular facilitator.
3. The facility in which the group is meeting may determine that it must withdraw the availability of space, alter the meeting schedule significantly, or modify membership criteria by requiring that everyone in the facility attend.

4. Membership may be mixed poorly in terms of values and how they see the world.
5. Group members may be unable to take responsibility for the group. In a sense, members under these circumstances may experience "existential angst," not really knowing why they are meeting together in the first place. Their limited commitment to a self-help orientation in situations such as these and the direction of the group are apt to become progressively unfocused. Under these circumstances, members often feel they are there to be entertained rather than to be engaged in personal conflict resolution, problem solving, and empowerment.

THE SOWN TRAINING FUNCTION

SOWN program staff offer group facilitators 10 hours of training each year. It is provided in the form of training workshops available twice a year—once in the spring and once in the fall. Each 5-hour workshop is offered between 10:00 a.m and 3:00 p.m. so as to coincide with the senior citizen, off-peak, half-fare transportation program in the Philadelphia metropolitan area. The sessions are actually open not only to group facilitators but to group members, social work and activity site staff in housing residences and senior centers where groups operate, and volunteers as well. Given the range of participants, sessions frequently have both professionals and nonprofessionals in attendance, including individuals without high school diplomas and those holding master's degrees.

The sessions are led by SOWN group facilitators. Students and volunteers assist with registration and question answering. Clerical assistance from the SOWN central office is available as well. All participants receive packets containing the day's agenda; name tags, the SOWN brochure, and a recent newsletter; pertinent articles on self-help, aging, women, and group process; blank group session-plan forms; examples of actual session plans; and quotable remarks from individuals participating in SOWN self-help groups.

Training workshops aim to encourage facilitators to think about what it is they do, to create functional descriptions of their group responsibilities, and to identify and develop those skills and talents that will make them effective at what they do. Training is experiential in its orientation. Role-playing is an effective tool for demonstrating group problems and learning how to deal with particular issues associated with group functioning. Training focuses on session and topic plan development, problem solving, developing listening skills, and becoming informed about the qualities of older women as leaders, group process, and diversity issues.

For the sequence of a typical training session, see the boxed list that follows.

TYPICAL TRAINING SESSION

- Registration
- Greetings from the executive director of SOWN
- A get-acquainted exercise—This encourages participants to move around the room, meet each other, and get to know about different groups operating in the community. Commonly, participants are asked to pair off with someone they have never met and identify things they have in common with each other. Participants then report back to the larger group about what they have discovered.

- A formal presentation—This focuses on a particular special topic such as listening effectively, enhancing the power of the group, fostering group cohesion, the leader's role in the group, and challenges to leadership and group process. Much of this discussion draws directly from materials and content that are included in the SOWN training manual. Ultimately, these presentations touch on why older women join groups, what keeps people in groups, and how leaders can encourage group stability.
- Distribution of didactic materials related to the presentation
- Initial question and answer
- Break for lunch
- Continuing question and answer—The most common questions that arise from participants, especially those whose groups have been meeting for extended periods of time, tend to be requests for assistance in developing ideas for group session topics. Staff focus their efforts on helping facilitators and group members develop their own techniques for determining what topics a group will discuss.
- Topic development brainstorming session—This session is held in such a manner as to ensure that everyone's ideas for topics are accepted. During the brainstorming session, it is established policy that negative comments will not be made regardless of the topics suggested. The process usually results in a full-page listing of potential group topics. The point of the process is not simply to arrive at a new list of topics but to learn the value of brainstorming as well.
- Session plan development—A topic of interest to the group is chosen, and the various elements of a session plan are developed through mutual discussion. Elements of a facilitator's standard session plan include an introduction to the topic; open-ended questions that will stimulate, encourage, and maintain discussion; and summary comments. Session plans aim to set the stage for a group meeting, instigate and keep a discussion going on a particular topic, and summarize the proceedings. All participants depart from a training session with one complete session plan.
- Problem solving—At the beginning of the day, all participants present problems they are experiencing in their self-help support groups. Common issues raised include the disruptive group member, members who dominate the discussion, the death of a member, and group member disagreement regarding the topic or subject matter to be addressed on a given day. Training workshop participants break into groups and are given a problem that was identified anonymously earlier in the morning. Everyone has an opportunity to participate in role-playing or small-group activities during which the particular problem is addressed. Strategies and solutions are devised in the small groups for dealing with the problem, and these are presented to all attendees at the training session. Staff make an effort to make these problem-solving groups quite diverse in terms of the profiles of participants.
- Closing and business

Facilitators are invited but not required to attend training workshops. Approximately 25–35 facilitators participate each year in the training sessions, representing a little more than half of all facilitators associated with SOWN groups.

Experiential workshops are also offered periodically to groups in the community. In the past, these sessions have dealt with such topics as aging stereotypes; empowerment, self-esteem, and self-image issues; and the fear of growing older.

DESCRIPTION OF A TYPICAL SOWN MEETING

Most groups have some kind of agenda. However, it is important to understand that preestablished agendas are not always adhered to. For most, the major concern each week seems to be the welfare of the group. If anyone has a problem to share or resolve, this is discussed initially. Following this, the group might have a speaker or proceed with the assigned topic. There are some differences in operating procedures, often depending on whether the facilitator is a staff member or a peer. Specifically, indigenous leaders are more likely to feel that it is their job to decide on the topics a group will deal with on a given day. They are then likely to concentrate their efforts on encouraging the group talk about the designated topics. Staff facilitators, however, seem to defer more to the group and act primarily as monitors of group process.

Two groups have the tradition of beginning and ending with a prayer. Three groups have guest speakers on a regular basis; two of these are groups within structured retirement communities. One of the groups ends with a song composed by the group facilitator:

> *The best of times is now*
> *We get together and we talk things out—*
> *We're friends who show support—*
> *With happy hearts*
> *We know the best of times is now.*

Most of the members are inclined to speak about what happens in a typical group gathering in terms of topics discussed: family issues, childhood memories, life in general, politics, health, raising children, cooking, theater, or just how things used to be. However, the most widely discussed topic appears to be current events.

The primary focus in any given group on any given day is on how the members feel, what problems they wish to discuss or resolve, and what happened during the previous week.

One group changed its name to "For Women Only," making it quite clear who was eligible to participate and who was not. Another group met on a monthly basis with the men's group at the center. Groups thus appear to be of different opinions about the extent to which meetings should be limited to older women, although certainly the vast majority of meetings consist exclusively of older women. However, group participants seem to be in general agreement that they do not like to discuss anything sad or painful, unless it is necessary to help a group member to cope with a profound loss or a serious problem.

One member noted how the leader used a plastic bowl containing slips of paper containing ideas for topics. For example, one such topic is "your most embarrassing moment." Another cited a special Mother's Day meeting, where "someone did some research on famous mothers in history. She gave each of the women a part to read."

One woman sums up the format as follows:

> *We'd be seated in a circle, and we'd go all around and everyone would give their thoughts and opinion on that subject. Sometimes it would be controversial. You got to know people better from the exchange. You'd learn from people talking about their life experience. People would talk about religious convictions, fears, philosophical convictions—things that wouldn't come up in daily conversation.*

Successful and Meaningful Topics

As described in chapter 3, the range of topics discussed by SOWN groups is impressive. This section provides an analysis of those topics and subject matter and considers which have realized greater and lesser degrees of success.

Facilitators' Views. Almost universally, facilitators have indicated that group members prefer to address positive and upbeat topics and resist talking about death and losses. Family and health seem to be the most prevalent topics mentioned. Other popular topics include travel experiences, friendship, current events, widowhood, and everyday living. A few of the groups are also interested in political issues and determine numerous topics based on newspaper articles, especially concerning the American Association of Retired Persons and features on aging.

One of the groups led by the staff facilitator does problem solving regularly and defines itself as a support group, as opposed to a social group, as some of the groups see themselves. An example of the latter focus is implied in the following comment: "It's just people meeting in the living room and chatting—1 hour of getting together."

Most groups, however, do have some meetings that can become very emotional. One facilitator related the following experience:

> *The most meaningful [topic] is hard to say. Except once we had a Valentine heart [when _____ was leader] and she made us pass it around. She asked who we would put in this heart. She asked us to relate to the heart. I put my grandmother in. Some cried and it was touching.*

The same facilitator sums up the most liked and disliked topics, respectively: how to grow old gracefully and losing your independence.

Some of the more popular topics cited by group facilitators include feelings, raising children, African American history, Medicare legislation, living wills, world events, and material from talk shows, newspapers, and television news.

Group Members' Views. Numerous items were mentioned as most meaningful. Some common discussions centered on childhood memories, working days, and family problems. One member related how she was able to talk in the SOWN group for the first time about being abused by her father when she was a child. She became very emotional in telling her story again to the interviewer.

One member noted that both educational and emotional topics seem to elicit the most attention in terms of meaning. Bringing in items from the past, whether clothing or household things, also seems to provoke interest.

Other memorable topics noted by elder members of the groups include the following: life and death, church activities, a dietitian's talk, things that make you happy, discussion of a living will, the importance of friendship, "I am not alone," loss of a loved one, grandchildren, holiday customs, and entertainment.

Staff Views. SOWN staff have found, in general, that such topics as how to deal with loneliness and widowhood and life review (members' lives past and present) are most popular. Even so, the desirability of topics often depends on the group. In one group, for example, "anything introspective doesn't grab them." Groups in nursing homes, in particular, cannot deal as effectively with inferential, introspective questions. Some groups have chosen to set up ground rules agreeing not to talk about particular issues (e.g., politics, religion, anything unpleasant, sexuality, etc.).

Facilitator Characteristics and Views of Group Meetings

Group facilitators reported that their groups have been operating an average of 4.5 years. These particular facilitators, however, had performed in that capacity, on the average, for 2.5 years. The majority (10, or 71.4%) did not cofacilitate a group; that is, they were the sole facilitators during any given meeting.

Facilitators reported that their groups were likely to meet on a weekly basis (this was the case for 10 of 14 facilitators). The remaining groups meet either every other week or less frequently. When a facilitator was unable to attend a meeting, the responsibilities of facilitation were usually assumed by a group member.

Five of the facilitators (35.7%) considered themselves to be group members in terms of their affiliation. Seven of the women were agency employees situated at the site where their groups meet. Another woman categorized herself as a volunteer. Interestingly, the majority of these women had not facilitated a group before, nor had they been members of another support or community group. For many, the experience appeared to be a novel one.

The average group consisted of 13.5 members, although the sizes of groups varied considerably, ranging from as few as 5 to as many as 20 women. The average meeting was attended by 9 women. Four facilitators maintained that their groups consisted of women having no physical limitations (e.g., no members were in need of a cane or walker or had a heart condition that caused difficulties in terms of mobility). Almost two thirds (64.3%), though, indicated that fewer than 25% to 49% of their members had mobility limitations. It is clear that self-help support groups for older women are more likely than not going to include women in measurable numbers who are experiencing decline in some aspect of functional capacity. As a result, one can expect that decisions around where and when groups will meet will take on considerable significance, as will planning pertaining to ensuring access to acceptable modes of transportation for group participants.

Reflecting a pattern similar to group members, the vast majority of group facilitators appeared satisfied to restrict their responsibilities to that of operating the SOWN groups to which they were assigned. They expressed minimal interest in engaging in such other SOWN activities as making TV and radio appearances, doing office work, attending health fairs, or sitting on committees and boards. Apparently, group facilitation was responsibility enough for most of those women, who assumed such positions regardless of their health or functional status.

Members' Views of the Most and Least Liked Features of the Group

What aspects of SOWN group participation were seen as particularly satisfying? What features were less enjoyable? Table 5-1 summarizes the most and least liked features of SOWN. It is clear from these data that the most satisfying or enjoyable aspect of group participation was the opportunity to develop new friendships and socialize with other older women. This feature was mentioned by 70% of

Table 5-1 Group members' most and least liked features of their support groups

Feature	Yes		No	
	No.	%	No.	%
Most liked				
Friendship/socialization	158	70.0	68	30.0
Communication	77	34.1	149	65.9
Education/information	63	27.9	163	72.1
Emotional support	49	21.7	177	78.3
Other	8	3.5	218	96.5
Least liked				
Poor listening skills	18	8.0	208	92.0
Rudeness/inappropriateness of some members	11	4.9	215	95.1
Disorganized agenda	11	4.9	215	95.1
Not enough time	4	1.8	222	98.2
Poor participation	4	1.8	222	98.2
Topic choice	3	1.3	223	98.7
Other	7	3.1	219	96.9

respondents. Less frequently mentioned rewards, but nevertheless relatively common positive features of group participation, were opportunities to communicate with others, become better educated and informed on matters of managing in old age, and both providing and receiving emotional support.

It is notable that throughout the project women registered few examples of negative features of SOWN group involvement. Those features mentioned most frequently were the poor listening skills of certain group members, rudeness and inappropriate behavior on the part of some women, and somewhat disorganized agendas at certain group meetings. Less frequently mentioned dislikes included inadequate time at meetings to deal with particular issues, poor or uneven participation patterns among group members, and poor choices of topics dealt with from time to time.

Other data not reported in Table 5-1 add perspective in terms of those factors that have proved less satisfying for the participating women. Nineteen respondents indicated some dissatisfaction with the amount of time allotted for each member to be heard. Ten additional women felt not enough time was spent on certain issues, and 8 respondents felt the groups were not run as effectively as they might be. Program participants less often expressed difficulties with the timing and location of meetings.

Facilitators' Perspectives on Members' Needs

Group facilitators also offered suggestions as to selected other needs of participants in their SOWN groups. These included increased opportunities for self-expression, increased emotional support during difficult times, and, as needed, information and education.

Views of Group Discussion Topics

Group Members' Opinions. To gain an understanding of women's views of the value of SOWN group discussion topics, members were asked to indicate those topics that they found to be most helpful and those that they would like to talk about in their groups in the future. This information is summarized in Table 5-2. Friendships, current events, life review, relationships with children, communicating better, and health issues stood out as having been particularly helpful (in each case by at least 20% of the women). Similarly, in each case, 20% or more of the women

Table 5-2 Group members' opinions of discussion topics

Discussion topic	Most helpful topics				Desired future topics			
	Yes		No		Yes		No	
	No.	%	No.	%	No.	%	No.	%
Friendships	117	52.0	108	48.0	87	38.7	138	61.3
Current events	95	42.2	130	57.8	117	52.0	108	48.0
Life review	78	34.7	147	65.3	60	26.7	165	73.3
Relationships with children	69	30.7	156	69.3	46	20.4	179	79.6
Communicating better	69	30.7	156	69.3	64	28.4	161	71.6
Health issues	52	23.1	173	76.9	63	28.0	162	72.0
Grandparenting	40	17.8	185	82.2	31	13.8	194	86.2
Filling weekend time	38	16.8	188	83.2	40	17.8	185	82.2
Nutrition	36	16.0	189	84.0	53	23.6	172	76.4
Important women in my life	32	14.2	193	85.8	28	12.4	197	87.6
Living wills	25	11.1	200	88.9	39	17.3	186	82.7
Death and dying	21	9.3	204	90.7	17	7.6	208	92.4
Sexuality and older women	20	8.9	205	91.1	24	10.7	201	89.3
Memory loss	18	8.0	207	92.0	47	20.9	178	79.1
Relationships with spouses	16	7.1	209	92.9	9	4.0	216	96.0
Dreams and fantasies	14	6.2	211	93.8	16	7.1	209	92.9
Financial management	12	5.3	213	94.7	29	12.9	196	87.1
Housing	11	4.9	214	95.1	17	7.6	208	92.4
Legal issues	—	—	—	—	24	10.7	201	89.3
Other	5	2.2	220	97.8	9	4.0	215	96.0

surveyed wanted to talk more about each of these topics at a future meeting. In addition, matters pertaining to nutrition and memory loss were also proposed as future topics by at least one in every five respondents. In terms of both past helpfulness and future planning, strategies for developing and maintaining friendships and reviewing current events can be separated out as particularly popular themes.

Facilitators' Opinions. According to the facilitators, the topics covered most frequently in groups (75% or more of the time; in descending order) are life review, relationships with children, health issues, friendships, communicating better, and grandparenting. Topics covered between 50% and 75% of the time (in descending order) included current events, nutrition, important women in one's life, relationships with spouses, financial management, memory loss, housing, and death and dying. Topics covered in fewer than 50% of the groups included dreams and fantasies, sexuality, filling weekend time, and living wills. Topics mentioned as needing to be covered more than they had been included life appreciation and enjoyment and intergenerational relations.

CONCLUSION

By delineating major structural and strategic issues, it becomes apparent that the administration of an organization such as SOWN is necessarily complex, a fact that might not be so obvious to the casual observer of the self-help support groups. Well before the introduction of members at a first group meeting, significant effort has gone into the planning and preparation process. Careful attention to facilitator training, topic selection, and financial solvency is necessary to assure quality service provision and program survival.

Having considered a variety of factors intrinsic to the organization and operation of self-help support groups for older women, the analysis now proceeds to a presentation of the personal experiences of older adult members and facilitators engaged in group self-help. The next chapter aims, in effect, to chart the individualized views and opinions of older women and their facilitators engaged in the actual process of group self-help. Such data should offer valuable personal perspective that enriches the operational properties of self-help groups characterized in this chapter.

6

Patterns of Participation
and the Personal Process of Group Self-Help

This chapter provides data reflective of the nature, duration, and intensity of women's involvement in support group activities. Patterns of interaction with other women both within and outside of the support group are considered, as well as the manner in which program participants first found out about the SOWN program. Group members' perspectives on the meaning of self-help are also considered. Group facilitators' perspectives on group process, the experiences of group members, and their own views of their responsibilities as leaders are considered as well. As was the case in the preceding chapter, this chapter's intent is to present detailed and systematic data and critical commentary on various dimensions of the SOWN program first introduced in chapter 3.

INVOLVEMENT AND PARTICIPATION PATTERNS
OF GROUP MEMBERS

How Women Learn About SOWN

In what ways are women likely to learn about self-help programs? Are mass media approaches or more personalized outreach the method of choice? Given SOWN's experience, it quickly becomes clear that informal, personalized communications can be expected to play a pivotal role in women's learning about the presence of these kinds of groups in their communities and neighborhoods. Most frequently, it is a friend or confidant who tells the typical female participant about a SOWN group. Attending speeches and talks given by SOWN staff and group facilitators at senior centers, churches, synagogues, and housing residences have also proved to be relatively common ways of learning about the support groups. These face-to-face, interactive strategies in many cases are commonly supplemented by informational notices and announcements posted specifically at a community meeting place where a SOWN group is to be organized. Mass media strategies (newspaper, radio, TV, standardized flyers) have apparently been used less successfully as recruitment tools for the program.

The success of personalized outreach in attracting older women as potential participants in self-help group programming is not surprising given the track record of other human service organizations serving older adults. Although most human service programs do not depend on single strategies for marketing, they are likely to agree that face-to-face, individualized methods provide the greatest return on investment. Radio, television, and newspaper announcements have not replaced the need to meet elders, their relatives, and friends; other service providers; and the general public on their own terms through in-person outreach, group presentation, and discussion (Kaye, 1994, 1995a, 1996b).

As the following situations suggest, personal outreach may involve an existing group member or a referring professional. In the case of Ms. Henry, contact with her senior center social worker proved to be the critical point of linkage.

During an appointment with a senior center social worker for information on Social Security benefits, Ms. Henry freely shared concerns about her recent retirement. Reduced income, lack of daily interaction with colleagues and customers, loss of benefits, and the specter of awaking each day with no meaningful activities planned were among the concerns of this single woman in her 60s. The social worker had worked with other elderly female clients who had obviously benefited from self-help group membership and confidently encouraged Ms. Henry to pursue this avenue. He additionally introduced Ms. Henry to other group members to allow her to get an insider's perspective on the gains to be derived from participation.

In the case of Mrs. Williams, the thoughtful actions of a concerned member of her church proved crucial.

Mrs. Williams, despite marked osteoporosis, managed to attend church quite regularly. Although she rarely attended social functions or other church-sponsored activities, she invariably shared a few pleasantries with fellow congregants before and after services. Motivated by a recent self-help group discussion of menopausal health concerns and familiar with the curvature of the spine associated with osteoporosis, Mrs. Tessa approached Mrs. Williams after services one week to tell her about the useful information and support available through her mutual aid organization. After several weeks of discussing the possibility, Mrs. Williams agreed to attend a meeting to determine whether the group could fill a need for her.

Not only can fellow elders be excellent ambassadors for self-help groups, but they are also very likely to receive a positive response from the invited party. Not unlike other situations in life, people are more easily influenced by a satisfied consumer than a paid professional with a vested interest in maintaining or increasing membership.

Quality and Duration of SOWN Involvement by Members

Group members were asked a series of questions concerning the quality and duration of their involvement with SOWN groups. These data are summarized in Table 6-1. More than half (113, or 52.1%) have been participating in support group activities between 1 and 5 years. The vast majority (88.4%) reported attending at least half of the scheduled meetings, with 69% reporting attendance levels between

Table 6-1 Degree of member involvement with support groups

Involvement measure		Frequency	%
Length of involvement			
<1 month		5	2.3
1–6 months		31	14.3
6 months–1 year		36	16.6
1–3 years		67	30.9
3–5 years		46	21.2
5–7 years		23	10.6
>7 years		9	4.1
Rate of attendance			
Almost always	(75%–100%)	149	69.0
Very often	(50%–74%)	42	19.4
Sometimes	(25%–49%)	17	7.9
Rarely	(<25%)	8	3.7
Projected involvement			
<6 months		4	1.9
6 months–1 year		4	1.9
As long as I'm able		206	96.2

75% and 100%. Furthermore, there was almost unanimous agreement among respondents (96.2%) that they anticipated attending meetings into the future for as long as they were physically able.

There were no significant differences found in the group participation levels of African Americans and Whites in terms of length of involvement, rate of attendance, felt level of involvement, or desired level of involvement. However, it is interesting to note that Whites were found to have significantly less frequent contact with group members outside of meetings as compared with African American women. However, outside group contact levels with group members do not differ significantly when comparing the experiences of married women with the experiences of those who were widowed, separated, or divorced. Interestingly, married participants were found to be involved with SOWN for significantly longer periods of time. Yet, the married women's rates of attendance, levels of felt involvement, and desired levels of group involvement in the future did not vary appreciably from those of their nonmarried counterparts.

As noted earlier in the case of group facilitators, women participating as group members do not commonly have pronounced interest in engaging in programmatic activities beyond those directly associated with attendance at their SOWN group meetings. Fewer than 1 in 10 of these women expressed interest in participating in the planning of health fairs (9.3%), working on the organization's newsletter (6.6%), doing volunteer office work (4.4%), making TV and radio appearances on behalf of SOWN (4.0%), or sitting on the board of directors (2.7%) or the Networking Committee (2.7%). It would seem that other women, perhaps those not significantly involved in self-help group activities either as group members or facilitators, will need to be recruited to assist with these supplemental tasks associated with organizational operations. Given the degree to which functional limitations have an impact on the cohort of women engaged in SOWN and similar such programming, it may not be realistic to assume that many will be able to contribute to a wide range of programmatic aspects of the organization beyond those roles growing out of their personal participation in their own group.

Member Interaction Outside of the Meetings

Several questions in the survey of older women addressed the nature of the women's interactions outside of formal SOWN group meetings. Considerable contact is evidenced. Well over half of the survey respondents (70.8%) said they interacted with one or more other group members two or more times a month. The most common type of contact was over the telephone (43.3%), followed by eating meals together (33.9%), and common attendance at a social group (28.1%). Going out together on a trip was not uncommon either (19.2%).

It should be noted that external contact between group members is as likely to take place for reasons of relaxation or having fun as compared with dealing with a specific problem or issue experienced by the women. Furthermore, and this seems quite important, almost one in two women (48.6%) wished they could have more contact (by phone, in particular) with their fellow group mates. More is said about this in chapter 10.

As the following example demonstrates, a relationship often evolves from a functional focus—mutual support—to a social or recreational focus over a period of time.

Mrs. Tesman and Mrs. Bouvier did not know each other before their participation in the same self-help support group. During the first several months in the group together, they interacted only during group sessions, and their relationship focused solely on providing support for each other. Mrs. Tesman's husband resided in a skilled nursing facility, and her life revolved around daily visits and advocating on his behalf as he suffered from Alzheimer's disease. Mrs. Bouvier had been widowed a year prior. While sharing with group members the stresses inherent in her caregiving role, Mrs. Tesman noted that she did not drive and therefore had to take a bus to the facility where her spouse resided. Following the meeting, Mrs. Bouvier approached her, suggesting that, on occasion, she would be able to offer her a ride as she passed the facility whenever she drove to her hairdresser. Mrs. Tesman happily agreed, and the two found that they had much in common to discuss, both related to the areas in which they sought support and in complementary social and personal interests. They soon began meeting regularly for lunches and card games and ultimately became intimate friends.

At any stage of life, developing new friendships can be difficult. The potential risk of rejection involved in initiating a close relationship may be a deterrent to taking the first step. However, using a support group as a forum for meeting new people and gradually becoming increasingly familiar with one another reduces both the risk and the fear of reaching out to someone who does not wish to reciprocate. Facilitators and others involved in self-help group activities can assist in the development of outside friendships for those who are interested by identifying this as one of the potential benefits of group participation.

QUALITY OF THE FACILITATORS' EXPERIENCE

Group facilitators were asked to assess the quality of their own experiences as group facilitators. First, facilitators rated the helpfulness of a variety of factors in their leading groups. On the basis of their responses, it is quite clear that the greatest help for these women was the SOWN program newsletter, visits from SOWN staff, information from sources other than SOWN, and special help from SOWN staff when difficult problems arose. SOWN training sessions, general phone calls from SOWN staff, and general information received from SOWN was slightly less helpful. Of lesser help (and this is important) was the assistance that facilitators received from other members of the group in organizing and coleading the group as well as in developing topics for group discussion. Clearly, the professional resources of SOWN stand out as serving an important, if not crucial, function in the successful performance of the facilitators' group responsibilities. If SOWN is to be seen as exemplifying the self-help group experience of older women, then the pivotal function served by professional human service staff cannot be denied.

Facilitators were also asked to identify those aspects of group leadership that had proven to be particularly demanding. Clearly, thinking up new topics and dealing with group reaction to touchy topics or subject matter stand out as those aspects of group programming that are likely to be most demanding of the facilitators. Organizational and technical facets of operating a group (e.g., reminding members about meetings, assigning tasks, etc.) were less likely to be burdensome for the facilitators. Interestingly, least demanding for facilitators was dealing with extreme distress expressed by a group's membership (such as anger or sadness), addressing boredom felt by themselves or group members, and dealing with any criticism they might receive from the women. As the following example demonstrates, dealing with sensitive topics can be one of the most trying responsibilities for facilitators.

Mrs. Fletcher had been a self-help group leader for almost 2 years, yet the prospect of introducing and facilitating a conversation on sexuality was stressful. Her personal upbringing had taught her that ladies don't discuss or admit to sexual desires, a message that clung stubbornly despite enlightenment in later life. She knew that many other members shared such a background and would react with shock, embarrassment, or retreat. Yet, Mrs. Fletcher was acutely aware of the need to broach the topic as a few members had privately mentioned related concerns: a husband's impotence after starting a new prescription, sexual desire after being widowed, and disinterest in responding to a partner's advances. By introducing the subject matter with a brief review of her own upbringing and resulting discomfort to the present, she was able to lead into a discussion of the less threatening aspects of female sexuality in later life and, ultimately, address more intimate concerns. Her sensitive treatment of the topic, a willingness to take the risk of sharing personal information herself, and reassurances that the rules of confidentiality and unwavering support would be respected, resulted in a highly successful session.

It is important to note that facilitators were able to offer suggestions on ways in which their own stress associated with the responsibilities of group leadership could be reduced. First of all, it should be said that 4 of the 14 facilitators maintained they had no stress associated with operating the groups. Of greatest value in reducing facilitator-related stress when it does arise was participation of other members in the responsibility and process of developing meaningful topics, followed by participation by other members in coleading groups, visits from SOWN staff, and SOWN training workshops. Less commonplace strategies suggested by facilitators included general help from SOWN when problems occur, participation by group members in organizing the group, use of the SOWN newsletter, and receipt of general information from the SOWN program. Least valuable strategies were believed to be information from sources other than SOWN such as health and social service organizations; training from other self-help, health, and social service entities; and phone calls from SOWN staff.

Facilitators also offered their views as to those aspects of being a group facilitator that have proven to be most and least satisfying. As was the case for group members, it was made quite clear that the opportunities that group participation afforded for gaining support, building friendships, and enjoying the companionship of others far outweighed any problem-solving, educational, or informational rewards that were derived from group involvement. Least satisfying aspects of being a group facilitator included (in descending order of importance) trying to control instances of group dysfunction, having to carry too much responsibility, lack of participation by group members, and choosing appropriate topics for the group.

Facilitators admitted that they were least well prepared for dealing with hostility and personality clashes in the group, challenging group dynamics, and presenting certain discussion topics, especially those of a sensitive nature (e.g., those dealing with issues of sexuality or racial and ethnic diversity). Even so, these issues did not appear to represent overwhelming challenges for the majority of facilitators. None of the facilitators indicated that they had turned to the SOWN office for assistance in dealing with these issues.

Asked to judge the quality of their leadership expertise, the facilitators responding to this survey were more than twice as likely to assess themselves as somewhat effective rather than very effective at what they do. Furthermore, 9 of the 14 respondents admitted to needing anywhere from a little to a lot more training. Training needs centered on the demand for greater expertise in understanding and dealing with group dynamics and to a much lesser extent on developing topics and session planning. Five of the 14 facilitators indicated that they would like SOWN to provide increased direction in terms of the skills and techniques of group facilitation. The remainder are satisfied with SOWN's assistance in this regard.

FACILITATOR AND MEMBER PARTICIPATION PATTERNS IN SOCIALIZATION OUTSIDE OF THE SOWN MEETINGS

Apparently, it is quite commonplace for indigenous facilitators to find themselves interacting with group members in various ways and contexts outside of the formal group meetings. Only one of the facilitators who were interviewed saw members only at meetings. Most had some outside contact, whether at the senior center, in the same apartment building, or at church. Lunch seems to be a popular activity for mutual engagement among and between group members and facilitators. As a matter of practice, facilitators are encouraged to build outside relationships between themselves and group members and between group members themselves. One facilitator mentioned that she and another member vacationed on a cruise together. If possible, facilitators encourage group members to visit anyone who is sick, or at least to send a card or make a telephone call.

Only 8 of the 50 members participating in face-to-face interviews reported not seeing other members outside the group. For the remainder, the most common gathering place was at a senior center or similar such community gathering place where the support groups meet. Other places where group members found opportunities to interact with each other included churches and synagogues, shopping centers, each other's homes, and the congregate housing residences (for those in communal living arrangements) where meetings are convened. And, finally, many of the older women maintained telephone contact, whereas a few met regularly for lunch or dinner. Although it was not particularly commonplace, for those members who were exceedingly close, trips were taken together.

Members' Involvement in Other Small Groups

In chapter 4, it was discovered that group members had had rather limited experience with support group involvement before their participation in SOWN. To what extent did these women also limit their involvement in group activities of a more general nature before discovering SOWN? That is, are the older women who engage in self-help group programming involved substantially in other types or categories of group function? Is the self-help group experience simply a continuation of an established pattern of participation by these women in other nonsupportive type group activities? Or does self-help participation represent a new and novel adventure by these individuals into the experience of organized group programming?

It was discovered early on in this investigation that, although not particularly extensive, some of the women had had rather interesting previous experiences with non–support-type groups, including participation in such organizations as the National Organization of Women, Action Alliance, tenant councils, neighborhood groups, and senior center group activities. It appears that these women had made decisions to focus their involvement either in large national or regional bodies or in local groups associated with local community programs. Seldom did women describe involvement in both categories of groups (national and local). The predominant type of general group experience noted by the women talked to proved to be an association with a local religious organization, whether it was a church, synagogue, or Bible study group. Three women stated they had some involvement in group and family therapy, and one had been attending a codependency group. Other diverse examples of previous group experiences included choral groups, intergenerational groups, Retired Senior Volunteer Program, Jewish War Veterans' Auxiliary, Older Women's League, and historical meetings. As noted in chapter 4, these women's experiences with groups explicitly geared to providing support was extremely limited. Ten members reported having had no contact whatsoever with any other group or association.

The primary difference between the other groups these women were affiliated with and SOWN support groups appears to be the personal tone set by the latter—the opportunity to be just with women and to talk about what bothers women. These women, in large part, perceived SOWN to reflect an atmosphere wherein true friendships are born and nourished. It is there that they could "let their hair down," learn how to cope with growing old and how to adjust to the increasing losses in their individual lives, and, finally, how to express feelings that might be buried and otherwise never expressed.

Most women noted a distinct and welcome difference with SOWN, highlighting the following characteristics: personal, individual, private, focused on women's issues, and open to women only. "With SOWN it spreads in different directions from a nucleus." It is the "[shared] feelings as opposed to common interest or external things" that makes SOWN different.

EFFECTS OF DIVERSITY ON THE GROUP

Facilitators' Views

Most of the facilitators stated that differences among group members really did not affect the group. This appears to be the case in large part because many of the groups were, for the most part, largely homogeneous regarding marital status, religious affiliation, and cultural background. As a consequence, an immediate closeness can be observed based on the commonalities that arise out of the homogeneity of the group.

The staff facilitators may have been able to be more objective or else more analytic in addressing this issue than their counterparts (the indigenous facilitators or peer leaders). In fact, staff facilitators proved to be of the same mind in highlighting the challenges to effective group function. The challenge, in their view, was brought on by sometimes divisive differences in terms of members' personalities, cultural and religious backgrounds, socioeconomic status, and personal values and norms. In one of these groups, the women lived together in the same building, and sometimes the problems of the community in which they lived were carried over to the SOWN meeting and had to be processed with the help of the social worker–staff facilitator.

The peer leader who became a staff person mentioned that in her group, several of the women were wheelchair bound. Apparently, there is sometimes resentment directed toward these members. She explained the dynamics as follows:

All add to the group—the variety, the disability. Well persons feel ashamed of themselves, and it balances out and makes everyone equal. When we see a handicap, it gives us a sense of our own mortality. Some are affected too much and are not ready to face it. In some ways they see themselves there and are not ready to cope with that possibility or probability.

Group Members' Views

The majority of the members interviewed actually expressed the belief that differences did not negatively influence the group but, rather, enhanced it. Ten women, however, saw some problems with diversity in the following areas: age, physical handicap, marital status, and financial status. It was noted by some of the married women in particular that they were made to feel uncomfortable in the group because their husbands were still living. Most members in a given group reflected a relatively common financial status, but there were a few exceptions where variations in financial well-being among the older women in a particular group have been known to lead to difficulties. The following example demonstrates conflict arising from dissimilarities.

> *The vast majority of members of a particular self-help support group for older women were widowed, which, one might assume, would provide a strong foundation of commonality. On closer inspection, however, it was apparent that subgroups existed. In particular, there were those who had been widowed for approximately 2 years or more and, at the other extreme, those who were very recently widowed. The former group, who themselves had admittedly benefited from peer support in the early days of widowhood, now wanted to focus on issues such as building new social relationships, planning recreational activities, and just getting on with life. Many felt weighed down by the recent widows in the group who needed to talk about the pain of loss. They didn't want to be forced to relive that period that they had survived and grown beyond despite the fact that they understood the other women's need for support and encouragement. There was even talk of breaking into two groups on the basis of marital status and duration of widowhood.*

In general, however, most groups were homogeneous or, at least, felt they were all in the same boat, coping with the trials and tribulations of aging gracefully. As the following example demonstrates, most self-help support group members preferred to focus on similarities.

> *Because aging is not an experience exclusive to any particular socioeconomic group, self-help groups for older persons typically attract women with varying financial capacities. Although income and assets were never directly addressed in the group in question, passing comments about vacations and recreational activities, as well as visible status symbols such as jewelry and designer clothing made most members aware of the general financial well-being of their peers. Any lurking jealousies or feelings of superiority were quickly dissipated when discussions of arthritis, widowhood, and relationships with children revealed that shared hardships and joys were unaffected by material resources. The perceived benefits of sharing common experiences and support clearly outweighed any desires to focus on dissimilarities.*

OLDER WOMEN'S PERCEPTIONS OF SELF-HELP

Facilitators' Views

A few facilitators had apparently never heard of (or did not remember) the concept of self-help, although when it was explained to them, they admitted they had been operating in that manner. Those who offered their perspectives on the meaning of self-help referred to being independent, "sharing your experiences like a 'sounding-board'," "trying to improve something in your life," or "being resourceful and finding ways to use what is available to you." In terms of how the group functioned, approximately one of every two facilitators believed that self-help was a pivotal part of the process.

Group Members' Views

Admittedly, quite a few members seemed to be vague as to the meaning of self-help. Most knew what it meant after it was explained, but did not know whether their group should be classified as such. Most of the responses centered on "helping yourself and doing things for yourself," or being independent. Variations on this definition included the following: "Have a check on yourself;" "learn how to do things for yourself;" "get someone to take an interest in herself;" and "have faith and comfort in yourself."

One member summarized it as follows: "Mingling with people who have experienced the same things, companionship and friendship—knowing that people are going to be there."

GROUP FACILITATORS' PERCEPTIONS
OF THE LEADERSHIP ROLE

Excluding the two staff facilitators, the group facilitators assumed the leadership position in various ways. Two were chosen by the SOWN office representative, two volunteered, and two filled in temporarily and then became permanent. Only one seemed to be inherently excited about holding the facilitator position, although most said it was rewarding. One noted that "being a leader is part of me."

Some of the skills cited for being a good facilitator included the ability to get along with people, flexibility, patience, tolerance, a nonjudgmental attitude, compassion, listening skills, and understanding. One facilitator noted the importance of "[loving] people and loving working with them. Everyone is different and sometimes it's really trying to deal with envy, jealousy and judgmental attitudes. I didn't feel prepared in the beginning, but I learn as I go along."

A self-help group facilitator for several years, Ms. Wesley regularly finds herself challenged by her role and advises that the qualities of patience and tolerance are of considerable import. Over the years, members who are particularly reluctant to participate or open up have tried her patience as they often hold back group cohesion. Gentle encouragement has achieved far greater results than the more tempting technique of public confrontation regarding a lack of input. Far more members have promoted opinions and philosophies that run contrary to her own. Particularly with regard to advice extended by participants to peers, Ms. Wesley has had to develop her sense of tolerance to allow for suggestions that are in opposition to her own. Despite an intellectual recognition of the value of diverse opinions, her ability to withhold criticism of those with dissenting views has developed with great difficulty but positive results.

The ability to speak and take over a group is also considered important. Another woman highlighted the importance of leadership meetings and the need for SOWN staff to visit the centers to help with this type of training on site. There apparently are mixed feelings on the adequacy of the training. Six were hesitant to take a stand and make a comment; three admitted it was not adequate, especially in terms of length of time offered. It was generally felt that 8 weeks was not enough. The demands of self-help group facilitation clearly are considerable. Those who assumed the responsibility recognized the need to be prepared beforehand as well as during the course of the experience in order to carry out facilitation tasks successfully.

One leader who spoke positively regarding the training sessions noted that the "training was excellent, but it's hard to get women to utilize the training to run the group. Some see it as a burden. They are tired and it's too much stress. There's responsibility away from the center."

The majority of group facilitators agreed that the members commonly assist them in their respective roles as facilitators. Only two facilitators dissented from that perspective concerning the helpfulness of members. They warned that jealousy felt by members because of the enhanced status achieved by women filling the role of facilitator can be a problem of considerable proportion, inhibiting many from willingly assisting facilitators in ways that would otherwise have been helpful and certainly appreciated. One facilitator who was having problems with her group noted a lack of consideration and responsibility on the part of members who did not take commitment to the group seriously.

> *I think the SOWN group should work together—I think each should put more effort forward to make the group more friendly to each other. It says if a member isn't going to be there, she should call and let us know, and I have yet to receive a call. It says something about them contributing topics and effort—I haven't seen that done. I compare it to other groups—maybe I expect too much of them.*

As was noted in the discussion of the demanding aspects of group leadership earlier in this chapter, there are diverse challenges to successfully running a support group for older women. To summarize, they include personality conflicts; development of topics; facilitation of the group when emotional issues arise, such as the death of a member; and maintenance of ground rules for the group, especially centered around listening skills. Finding enough topics over the long term also seems to be a predominant problem or challenge. A combination of a lack of experience and a lack of training are repeatedly cited as causes of the difficulty faced in meeting the challenges outlined above, creating the feeling of not being prepared to handle sensitive and emotional situations.

It is not uncommon to find one group member who consistently tries to monopolize the conversation. Typically, such a person is one who speaks up to flaunt her own knowledge and highlight her own experiences rather than to help others. As the following example demonstrates, a trained and skilled facilitator can often manage such a challenge without alienating the talkative member.

> *Mrs. Katz had served as the facilitator of a fairly stable and cohesive group for over a year and a half when a new member, Mrs. Morris, joined. Initially, the members and facilitator did not object to her frequent input, as the problem with most new members was typically a reluctance to participate. Additionally, she indicated that she had belonged to other support groups in the past and felt that she could use her experience and knowledge*

to help this group. Within a few weeks, it became quite apparent to all involved that Mrs. Morris was primarily interested in being the center of attention, had a very inflated sense of self, and had little ability to really hear the true concerns of other participants. Soon, when she would begin to speak, others would roll their eyes or just look desperately at Mrs. Katz as if asking for help. After formulating a game plan, Mrs. Katz approached Mrs. Morris after a meeting and asked if she could have a few words with her in private. The facilitator skillfully appealed to the member's need to be recognized and began by indicating how much she appreciated having such a helpful, well-spoken woman in the group. She went on to note that not all the other women were equally capable of commanding the attention of others and articulating their concerns. Suggesting that she and Mrs. Morris were partners of sorts in their mutual quest to help the group, Mrs. Katz asked for her help in compiling a list of ground rules. These rules would be presented to the group as possible "norms of behavior" that they could discuss and vote on. The list, which included keeping communications appropriately brief, not interrupting others, and listening intently, was readily adopted by the group. Because of her role in the development of the norms, Mrs. Morris tried to comply immediately. When she strayed from the rules, others felt comfortable correcting her, as they did with other women who erred as well.

The tendency by some rather narcissistic members to dominate group process is certainly not the only challenge associated with members' personalities that faces facilitators. For example, one facilitator noted the potential difficulties arising from resentment that may be felt by able-bodied members toward members with handicaps. This facilitator pointed out that it is hard work to help the "well" members "see that they shouldn't take this [handicap] personally in their own lives."

CONCLUSION:
FINAL COMMENTS ABOUT THE SOWN EXPERIENCE

Throughout the interviews with group facilitators, the importance of SOWN staff from the main office visiting the sites on a relatively frequent basis was repeatedly emphasized. It was also suggested that there might be more "intermingling" among the SOWN groups throughout the city, not just to meet new people, but also to learn more ways of running the individual groups and to discover new topics and ideas. Several facilitators emphasized the importance of SOWN becoming more involved in training, especially in group dynamics, orientation for new members, communication skills, and the reorganization of groups that have been discontinued.

This chapter closes on a positive note with the enthusiastic response of one member who stated,

I feel they [SOWN] are doing a fabulous job. I feel this is something that can help all women get in touch with themselves and who they are. We need each other to put down the old stereotypes. We have to recognize the fact that just because we're gray, we don't have to be tired.

7

Impact of Self-Help Groups

QUALITY OF THE GROUP EXPERIENCE

To what extent do participants in the SOWN program derive comfort and satisfaction from the experience? Is group participation more helpful in dealing with one set of life challenges and crises than with another? This chapter considers the quality of the group experience as well as the relationship between the nature of that experience for members and selected sociodemographic and group participation variables. Data are also presented that reflect the quality of the facilitators' experiences with SOWN programming. Drake and D'Asaro, in chapter 3, asserted that the SOWN group experience is an exceedingly satisfying one for both participants and facilitators. Data presented here buttress that argument.

The Group's Influence on Members and Facilitators

To what extent does group involvement alter the lives of both facilitators and members? That is, is group participation an enlightening experience for them? One facilitator who was interviewed related how much the group has changed her personality from being very quiet and reserved to being outgoing and talkative. This facilitator felt as if she has been transformed and was obviously very pleased with her "new self." Staff facilitators have also remarked on how much the group has taught them about themselves and how they have learned to view their lives from the perspective of growing old.

It is apparent that several of the women participating in the groups have natural leadership ability but before their involvement in group activities had never been provided the opportunity to use it. Most convey a sense of how the group enriches their lives and how they are experiencing a "shared aging feeling."

One of the groups maintains a roster of approximately 18 members, most of whom attend on a regular weekly basis. Listening to the manner in which the facilitator describes her group makes it quite clear why the group is so stable in terms of its operations and rate of participation. The facilitator exudes a warm and caring feeling toward the women in the group and is solicitous about those who are not present. Without fail, she calls every absent member immediately after each group meeting. In doing this, she is able to check to see if members who were not in attendance are physically well, and she is able to keep them informed of new developments arising from the group meeting.

Another facilitator noted that belonging to the group

> has made [her] more conscious of the generation gap and aware of examples of age discrimination around her. I find that interviewers in a mall asking your opinion about [some product] aren't interested in what you have to say as soon as they hear you are a certain age. It's like your opinion doesn't matter, and it's the same with people calling up and asking things on the phone. I think it's kind of shocking.

Ten members included among those interviewed stated the group has not, as yet, affected the way they see themselves. The remainder of the responses from participants were varied, including declarations that group participation has brought about changes in personality, as well as in philosophical thinking. Illustrative responses included "I am not alone—others have the same feelings and problems" and "I am never too old to learn." Others have expressed that they have realized a variety of insights as a consequence of group participation, including a better understanding of people, an improved perception of self, the realization that their ideas are important, and the refusal to become "a victim of age." The most common of personal quality changes resulting from group participation included increased confidence and a reversal of shyness.

One member summarized it poignantly:

> I think that our society categorizes women, mother, caretaker, widow—you're this gray person without a man, helpless, adrift, it's a very poor image—what SOWN does is give you back this feeling of dignity and importance. You can do anything and everything you want to do, you can be an achiever. Before you had your identity through your husband.

Expressions of this kind drive home in no uncertain terms the capacity of the support group to empower its individual members and increase their capacity to function, survive, and even thrive on the basis of their own capacities.

SOWN staff find it difficult to generalize in terms of a characteristic profile of an older woman who is most likely to gain from SOWN activities. On the one hand, women who live alone would likely benefit particularly well from attending a SOWN group. Yet, women have to want to engage in the group—to be a part of the group—to reap the rewards. In the final analysis, it may depend most, according to one staff person, on what the woman brings to the group as a result of her experience with family, friends, and other groups.

Satisfaction, Involvement, and Comfort Levels of Members

SOWN members' views were assessed on a series of quality-of-group-experience variables. It is clear from these data that the experience has been a positive one for most women. More than three quarters (75.7%) reported being "very satisfied" with their SOWN group. An additional 43 respondents (19.7%) were "somewhat satisfied." Only 10 respondents reported any degree of dissatisfaction with their groups. Furthermore, the vast majority of women said they felt either "very involved" (46.8%) or "somewhat involved" (46.9%) with the activities of their groups. Similarly, 86% of respondents were either "very comfortable" or "somewhat comfortable" with sharing their experiences with their groups. In the case of comfort levels, it is probably notable that 31 women (14%) did admit to feeling anywhere from moderate to severe discomfort in sharing their personal lives and circumstances with others in the group setting. As expected, verbalization of personal issues and problems was not a simple task for a number of these women. It did not, however, keep them from continuing to attend meetings.

Data indicate that more than 8 in 10 women (84.5%) are participating at their desired level of involvement in SOWN group activities. It is noteworthy, however, that of those who wished a different level of involvement, the wish to be more involved in group program functions was much more pronounced than the desire for lesser involvement (12.7% compared with 2.8%, respectively).

Subgroup analyses of the experiences of White and African American women as well as those married and not married at the time of the survey revealed high levels of agreement in terms of the perceived quality of the SOWN group experience. There were no measurable differences on seven separate measures of quality of the group experience when comparing married older women with widowed, separated, and divorced older women. Similarly, White and African American women reported consistently similar experiences in this regard save for the degree of help received from their SOWN groups during periods of emotional change or fluctuation. In this case, African Americans reported receiving significantly more support from their groups than did their White counterparts.

Relationship Between Quality of the Experience, Participation Levels, and Demographic Profiles of Members

A separate analysis was carried out comparing the relationship between respondents' quality of group experience and extent of group participation. These results are presented in Table 7-1. As shown, more frequent attendance is significantly

Table 7-1 Pearson's product–moment correlations between selected quality of group experience and extent of participation variables

Variable	1	2	3	4	5	6	7	8
1. ATTEND	—							
2. SHARING	.15*	—						
3. INVOLV1	.26**	.36**	—					
4. SATISFD	.12	.12	.39**	—				
5. HELPED	−.08	.00	−.09	−.20**	—			
6. GPHELP1	.02	.14	.24*	.17	−.65**	—		
7. GPHELP2	.06	.26**	.28**	.30**	−.39**	.68**	—	
8. SUPPORT	−.13	−.06	−.05	−.20*	.40**	−.43**	−.39**	—

$*p < .05.$ $**p < .01.$

Note. ATTEND = percentage of time member attends SOWN meetings; SHARING = level of comfort felt by member in sharing experiences with group; INVOLV1 = level of involvement felt in group; SATISFD = level of satisfaction felt with group; HELPED = measurement of help received from group; GPHELP1 = measurement of helpfulness of group during specific life changes; GPHELP2 = measurement of helpfulness of group during emotional changes; SUPPORT = measurement of support in life since becoming a group member.

associated (albeit at relatively weak levels) with increased comfort felt in sharing problems with other group members, and with an increased sense of involvement with the group. Furthermore, an individual's comfort level in sharing experiences with others in the group is significantly associated with that person's perceived involvement level and the extent to which help had been received during a period of personal emotional change. Interestingly, increments in individual satisfaction with SOWN programming are significantly associated with increased help received from the group during times of personal emotional change (i.e., changes in feelings of happiness, loss, feeling cared for, self-worth, connectedness, interest in life) rather than during times of change in particular life circumstances (i.e., changes in income, marital status, living arrangements, proximity to children).

Further correlational analyses confirmed that educational attainment levels of women are negatively associated (albeit weakly) with help received from SOWN groups during periods of personal emotional change. That is, more educated women tended to feel they had received less help during emotional crises. Furthermore, women's personal income levels were negatively associated with satisfaction and involvement levels. That is, as income levels increased, women were likely to express lesser levels of felt involvement in groups and lesser degrees of satisfaction with their groups.

Multiple regression analyses were performed to identify those variables with the greatest explanatory power in predicting group satisfaction levels, comfort with sharing levels, and group involvement levels among participating women (dependent variables in the analysis).

The same set of independent variables was used in each of the analyses as well as in subsequent multiple regression analyses presented later. Independent variables considered can be categorized as either demographic variables or group participation variables. The demographic variables were as follows: age, race, education, individual household income, health status, major change in life in past year, and volunteer status. The group participation variables were contact with members outside of group, length of membership, frequency of attendance, and involvement in other groups. Individual household income levels proved to be the only significant predictor of SOWN group satisfaction levels. Higher satisfaction was registered by those members with lower reported individual incomes. Length of group membership and education were borderline significant predictors. Interestingly, longer periods of group membership and greater educational achievement were associated with decrements in satisfaction levels. Together, these three variables accounted for 25% of the variance in personal satisfaction levels.

Comfort levels in terms of sharing experiences in the group were significantly influenced by three variables: race, a major life change during the past year, and education. Age and participation in other groups proved to be of borderline significance in predicting comfort in sharing levels. African American women, those who had experienced a major life change, more educated women, and, to a lesser degree, older women and those who participated in other support groups could be expected to be more comfortable sharing their life experiences in the SOWN groups. Together, these five variables accounted for 44% of the variance in levels of comfort in sharing.

Degree of felt involvement in SOWN group activities was significantly influenced by five variables: race, age, frequency of attendance, education, and involvement in other groups. As with levels of comfort in sharing, African American women, older women, more educated women, and women who participated in other support groups had heightened involvement levels in SOWN groups. This time, frequency of attendance was also positively associated with influencing involvement levels. Together, these five variables accounted for 47% of the variance in felt involvement levels.

BENEFITS OF THE GROUP EXPERIENCE FOR MEMBERS

This section considers the relative effectiveness of SOWN group programming for the participating women from a variety of perspectives. Various aspects of group helpfulness are considered, including the degree and type of overall help received from the group, changes in support levels realized during group membership, sources of support, extent and type of help received during crises, specific personal gains realized, and the individual benefits derived from group membership. Together with data presented in the previous section, these findings further confirm the efficacy of SOWN group programming.

Group Helpfulness to Members During Life and Emotional Changes

Perspective as to the influence SOWN has had on its older adult membership is gained by understanding the motivating factors behind continued attendance at meetings. It is clear that for a large majority of women, the aim is, first and foremost, to derive opportunities to socialize with others and to receive positive support from peers. This motivating factor, which is the dominant response expressed by members, speaks to these women's wishes to maximize their chances to interact with others like themselves. The drive to become better informed or educated on specific topics would seem to be significantly less important than the desire simply to communicate with others on an intellectual level (see Table 7-2).

The kinds of life and emotional changes experienced by members during the past 12 months have already been described (widowhood proved to be the most common life change, followed by a decrease in income, and positive emotional changes such as feeling more connected, greater interest in life, and feeling happier outweighed negative emotional changes). When asked, respondents indicated that SOWN has proved to be equally helpful during both times of dramatic life change and emotional change. In each case, approximately 80% of women found SOWN to be either "very helpful" or "somewhat helpful" during these demanding times. Fewer than 1 in 10 women believed SOWN to have been "not very helpful" or "not at all

Table 7-2 Primary reasons for continued SOWN membership

Reason	Frequency	%
Socialization or support	128	68.1
Education or information	34	18.1
Communication	22	11.7
Other	4	2.1

helpful." Other data confirm that SOWN has, in fact, proved to be helpful most commonly in the very areas in which these women indicate they wish assistance. Thus, help is more likely to be received in the areas of friendship development and emotional support than in improving communication skills or educational and informational enhancement.

Sources of Support and Support Levels of Group Members

Almost two out of three group members (62.1%) maintained that they have realized increased support from a variety of sources since becoming a SOWN member (see Table 7-3). Most frequent increases in support have been realized in these women's relations with relatives and friends (indicated by 27.2% of respondents) and in terms of the degree of telephone contact with other SOWN group members (registered by 23.7% of those surveyed). Increases in the level of knowledge these women had of older adult services are generally less frequently cited but not uncommon (19.6%). Increases in personal knowledge of medical services, legal services, and financial services are considerably less likely to be acknowledged.

Multiple regression analysis serves to identify those variables best able to explain variation in the level of sources of support in life since becoming a group member. Three variables emerge as significant or near-significant predictors of source of support level. They are education, having experienced a major life change in the past year, and individual household income. More educated, lower income women who have experienced a major life change in the past 12 months can be expected to report having more sources of support in their lives since being group members. These three variables account for 37% of the variance in support levels.

Group Helpfulness During Members' Life Crises

Almost one third of those surveyed (31.6%) pointed out that their SOWN group had proved helpful during the past year in dealing with what they considered to be a crisis situation. For those willing to describe the nature of such crises, mental or physical health crises and the death of a loved one proved to be the most commonly

Table 7.3 Level of support in life since membership in SOWN

Measure of support	Yes		No	
	n	%	n	%
Experienced increased support since membership	90	62.1	55	37.9
Source of support				
Increased contact with relatives or friends	61	27.2	163	72.8
Telephone contact with group members	53	23.7	171	76.3
Knowledge of older adult services	44	19.6	180	80.4
Knowledge of medical services	27	12.1	197	87.9
Knowledge of legal services	19	8.5	205	91.5
Knowledge of financial services	12	5.4	212	94.6

cited situations. Other, less frequently cited crises included those associated with the deteriorating quality of a relationship with a significant other and the loss experienced when a relative, significant other, or confidant moved away. Consider the following examples.

> *To all who knew her, Mrs. Simon was an exemplary wife, caring for a husband whose health was rapidly deteriorating as a result of Parkinson's disease. Although his mental and physical symptoms required her to cater to his needs around the clock, Mrs. Simon remained a healthy and vigorous 72-year-old. Three years after his diagnosis, Mr. Simon died. Having lost her mate of nearly 50 years as well as the focus of her daily life, Mrs. Simon fell into a depression that alarmed her children and friends alike. She showed little interest in maintaining her previously immaculate appearance and lost weight as a result of a poor appetite. After much prodding by her physician and neighbor, she grudgingly joined her neighbor's support group for older women. Mrs. Simon was a rather passive member of the group, but absorbed enough to recognize that other women—women very much like herself—lost beloved spouses, yet went on to forge new, satisfying lives for themselves. Over time, she became close to two other group members with whom she would go out for lunch, shopping, or to a matinee.*

Unlike Mrs. Simon, Mrs. Washington brought considerable individual strength and capacity to her self-help group.

> *Mrs. Washington was not totally surprised to discover that she had breast cancer. With a sister who had had a radical mastectomy many years earlier and a mother who had died of the disease in her 40s, Mrs. Washington had never expected to reach her 60s, as she had, without being similarly afflicted. She had almost planned for this occasion, mentally mapping out her strategy: which hospital she would go to, under what conditions she would agree to chemotherapy, and what she would include in a living will. Additionally, she intended to join a self-help support group, as her sister had, to help her through the emotional demands of the treatment and possibly terminal prognosis. Given her understanding of the benefits of support group participation and her excellent interpersonal skills, Mrs. Washington was able to both give and receive help. Within a short period of time, many other members began to look to her for support, considering her a "Rock of Gibraltar" or strong shoulder to lean on. It was in her capacity as helper to others that she found her greatest solace and strength to handle the emotional demands of mastectomy and chemotherapy.*

As this example clearly illustrates, those who typically benefit most from group affiliation are those who are able to provide as well as receive support.

Gains and Benefits of Group Affiliation for Members

Table 7-4 summarizes the gains derived from SOWN group membership, according to the women themselves. As shown, the ability to listen to others better, building new friendships, and receiving support for being an older woman can be separated out as representing the most common gains of group participation. Approximately 50% or more of the women acknowledged gains of this nature. Once again, gains such as

Table 7.4 Group member gains from support group membership

Gain	Yes		No	
	n	%	*n*	%
Listening better	154	68.4	71	31.6
New friendships	149	66.2	76	33.8
Support for being an older woman	112	49.8	113	50.2
Handling stress	89	39.6	136	60.4
Self-confidence	83	36.9	142	63.1
Support for being me	80	35.6	145	64.4
Valuing the past	74	32.9	151	67.1
Saying yes and no	73	32.4	152	67.6
Handling loneliness	66	29.3	159	70.7
Dealing with family relationships	61	27.1	164	72.9
Finding health care	56	24.9	169	75.1
Facing issues of death and loss	52	23.1	173	76.9
Sense of accomplishment	47	20.9	178	79.1
Handling the blues	39	17.3	186	82.7
Awareness of myths and stereotypes as they affect my self-image	38	16.9	187	83.1

these would seem to parallel those factors that motivated these women to attend and remain with their SOWN groups in the first place. Such gains can be reasonably classified as affective and relational rewards of participation.

Secondary gains, in a domain that might be classified as individual and personal gain, were realized in the areas of handling stress more effectively, gaining self-confidence, valuing the past, saying yes and no, handling loneliness, and dealing with family relationships. Least frequent gains were acknowledged in such areas as finding health care, facing issues of death and loss, deriving a sense of accomplishment, handling the blues, and becoming more aware of the influence that myths and stereotypes of aging have on one's self-image.

Multiple regression analysis was performed to identify those variables with the greatest explanatory power in predicting personal gain realized as a result of group participation. The dependent variable in the equation was the extent to which respondents learned or gained the 15 different social and emotional abilities or skills as listed in Table 7-4. This index, the Gain Through Group Involvement Scale, is described in appendix A. The index proved to be moderately reliable, with a Cronbach's alpha of .79 (a measure of internal consistency of index items).

Race, education, and individual household income are significant predictors of changes in perceived levels of social and emotional gain. More precisely, being African American, having a higher level of education, and having a lower level of individual household income were predictive of registering greater increases in perceived social and emotional gain as a result of participating in a SOWN group. Once again, as was reported earlier in the context of other potential rewards of SOWN participation, race, income level, and education proved to be particularly useful correlates of the positive benefits to be derived from group membership.

Serving as a volunteer, better self-perceived health, and increased frequency of attendance at group meetings also assisted in explaining increased personal gain levels, but these independent variables fell short of being significant predictors. Together, these six variables explained fully 42% of the variance in personal gain levels. It is noteworthy that group member age, employment status, participation in other support groups, length of membership in a SOWN group, contact with members outside of the group, and major changes in life during the past year proved to contribute minimally to the explanation of variance in the dependent variable and were therefore removed from the equation.

Finally, group members were asked to specify what they liked about being in their SOWN group (see Table 7-5). These data provided final confirmation of the primary benefits to be derived from participation. Almost three quarters of the women (73.5%) pointed out that they liked the opportunities for finding friendship and companionship. This benefit proved to be the most common such reward of group involvement. Clear majorities of older women also pointed out that they liked the fact that sessions were interesting and that they had a chance to talk at the sessions. Once again, these women's responses tended to highlight the opportunity that these groups afforded them to interact and relate to others. Personal enhancement and knowledge acquisition were also important but clearly of secondary importance.

SOWN'S EFFECTIVENESS IN DEALING WITH FACILITATORS' AND MEMBERS' MAJOR LIFE CHANGES

Facilitators' Experiences

Most of the group facilitators stated that they had experienced no major life changes during the course of their involvement with a SOWN self-help support group. For those who had, the changes can be categorized in the following areas:

Table 7.5 Benefits of support group membership

Benefit	Yes		No	
	n	%	*n*	%
Companionship or friendship	166	73.5	60	26.5
Interesting sessions	147	65.0	79	35.0
A chance to talk	137	60.6	89	39.4
Feel better	112	49.6	114	50.4
Gain knowledge	109	48.2	117	51.8
Helping others	102	45.1	124	54.9
Something to do	102	45.1	124	54.9
Stay updated on activities	98	43.4	128	56.6
Decreased loneliness	85	37.6	141	62.4
Finding out about self	76	33.6	150	66.4
Get support at critical times	61	27.0	165	73.0
Other	14	6.2	212	93.8

death of a spouse or loved one; sickness of someone significant, whether family
member or friend; and the loss of an apartment or home, accompanied by having to
give away many belongings.

For those who suffered changes, SOWN was viewed as having helped them
cope, unwind, and discuss alternatives. One facilitator summed it up: "People [in
SOWN] who hadn't known you that long really come to your rescue."

Members' Experiences

Unlike facilitators, most members who participated in the one-on-one intensive
interviews had undergone some degree of change, whether it was categorized as a
major life change or as a disruption in their routine of living in the recent past. Thirty
members responded positively to this question in terms of experiencing a major life
change. Examples of some of these changes included death of a relative, personal
surgery or hospitalization, illness of self or family member, financial problems, nursing home placement, retirement, loss of children out of the home, and "just growing
older."

Almost unanimously, the women interviewed stated that SOWN did help them
to cope and adjust to major changes in their lives. One noted,

*I retired from my job—[SOWN] prepared me for retirement, [by] having a circle of
friends who were also retired that I could share friendships with. Some women were
recently grieving. I'm sure they must have found it helpful. It made me more compassion-
ate toward other women.*

SOWN AS A MEANINGFUL EXPERIENCE FOR THE OLDER WOMAN

Views of Facilitators and Members

*Sometimes it helps me more than it helps them—but I think everyone benefits in some way.
I've gotten so I appreciate the little steps and begin to take things in stride. There are some
trusting, helpful people that come to your rescue.*

Comments such as these represent the sentiments of many of the facilitators. It
was noted that SOWN is an enriching life experience as well as one that provides
valuable insight. It has "proven to me that I can still learn and retain at this age."

The majority of group members' responses pertaining to what made their support
group a meaningful experience centered around the benefits of people and sharing,
including companionship, closeness, and friendship. Several women also remarked
on how much the facilitators meant to them. Commitment to the group, different
ideas, support, and activity were the remaining items cited as factors contributing to
a meaningful experience.

*I can express myself. I don't feel threatened. The different personalities [of other group
members] make it interesting to me. I feel I learn a great deal because of the different backgrounds. [I] really enjoyed meeting with other SOWN groups, [and] it was*

fascinating and enlightening to meet different people who were experiencing many of the same things.

Certain support group members actually reported a specific moment of realization when they, and perhaps others simultaneously, became aware of the sense of belonging and deep connection that comes from common experience and understanding. As highlighted below, it may be a moving experience for those involved.

Ten women had been meeting weekly since the group's inception 3 months prior. Although there were, at times, conspicuous lulls in conversation and difficulties in coming up with topics, members made a concerted effort to find common ground. On Mother's Day, participants agreed to discuss memories of their mothers from youth. This led to a more general conversation about the desire to be nurtured and loved, a need that they agreed remained into later adulthood. One woman, holding back tears, said she felt very much alone in this regard and longed for someone who really cared about her and whom she could count on. A peer immediately replied, saying she cared and would be very pleased to be able to help her. Several women openly cried, and some took each other's hands. It was on this day that the group was truly born.

CONCLUSION

Although there are discernable differences among subgroups of older women with regard to comfort levels with sharing experiences with the group and perceived social and emotional gain, overall, group members report high levels of satisfaction with their quality of group experience. Group affiliation is perceived as helpful during life changes and crises and is viewed as a useful venue for building new friendships.

In chapter 8, specific benefits and challenges of a national sample of self-help support group programs are presented. The organizational and strategic foundations that are necessary for the levels of satisfaction described in the current chapter are assessed.

8

Self-Help Support Group Programs in the United States

This chapter presents the results of a national comparative analysis of a select group of self-help support programs for older adults. Although all the groups studied are listed with local self-help clearinghouses, the term *self-help* does not appear in their brochures or literature. Groups are more commonly referred to as support groups or peer support groups. The purpose of this phase of the research was to develop a national database of information about the special benefits and drawbacks of existing program efforts at social network building for older women throughout the United States.

A range of current strategies and methods used and recommended by self-help and gerontological program planners and providers throughout the country were assessed. Information was collected by means of (a) a national review of selected research and program reports on alternative versions of self-help group programming and social network building for older adults generally, and older women in particular, and (b) in-depth interviews with a national panel of self-help and gerontological experts engaged in self-help and group services programming. Information collected centered around the following issues: (a) the characteristics of elder programs that emphasize self-help delivery and the strengthening of social support networks; (b) the critical factors that promote successful involvement of older women in self-help group programs; (c) the range of methods and techniques used in providing formal self-help delivery programs for older women; (d) the differences, if any, in programming strategies used by organizations in serving particular groups of older women varying in age, race or ethnicity, education, and presenting problem; (e) the specific targets of self-help programming for older women; (f) the type and extent of resources (funding, staffing, time) required to operationalize the self-help delivery model; (g) the training and expertise required of those bearing responsibility for mounting self-help groups in community service organizations; and (h) the identification of those program approaches and methods that have proven to be most effective in providing older adult self-help services.

A broad array of self-help program models was discovered. Some self-help

Deborah Feinhold took lead responsibility for conducting the national survey of self-help support group programs and preparing an earlier version of this chapter for the original technical report.

programs are large in scope, facilitated by trained volunteers and professionals, and part of larger institutions providing health, mental health, senior, or women's services. Other programs are smaller, more informal grassroots efforts organized by individuals or sectarian institutions such as churches and synagogues.

The goal of these self-help groups appears to be universal: to help the older person live a full and meaningful life and to provide an environment where older adults can support one another as they face the many physical, social, and spiritual challenges related to growing older in our society.

In the past 20 years, self-help support groups for older women have become a necessary and viable means of countering isolation, loneliness, and depression in older women in American society. Many self-help groups exist to deal with one particular challenge or problem. For example, caregivers' groups, widows' groups, or chronic pain groups reach out to elderly people experiencing a specific loss, disruption, or challenge. Peer support groups such as those studied here encompass these and many other issues. Older people are invited not to consider and focus on just one facet of their lives, but to confront the many issues that accompany the aging process.

This phase of the project concluded that existing self-help programs are largely successful in providing older adults with an important forum where they receive much-needed support. However, it is less clear whether these programs facilitate social network building for older women outside of the group environment.

THE APPROACH TO COLLECTING THE INFORMATION

Fourteen intensive telephone interviews were carried out with self-help program planners, developers, and leaders representing a variety of self-help program models in geographically diverse locales throughout the United States. This section describes (a) how self-help groups were identified and (b) how interviews were conducted with each expert associated with a self-help group. Persons to be interviewed were asked to submit materials associated with their programs, including brochures, articles, and training manuals. The information extracted from this material together with the information gleaned from the telephone interviews appears in the Findings from the National Survey section of this chapter. The Conclusion section presents a best practice model that describes the most common and successful approaches to providing self-help support groups for older women. This model may be used and adapted by programs throughout the country that are interested in providing this service.

Locating Groups

Self-Help Clearinghouses and Information and Referral Services. The National Self-Help Clearinghouse, located in New York City, provided the names of self-help clearinghouses and information and referral services located in various states throughout the country. Note that in this national survey, the term *self-help support group for older women* was defined as a group that brings together women on the basis of their advancing age and that addresses all of the varied and complex issues associated with aging. Groups that focus on a particular problem experienced by some older people, such as caregiving for sick parents, widowhood, or Alzheimer's disease, were not considered for this study. Clearinghouses were contacted in the following 19 states: California, Connecticut, Florida, New York, New Jersey, Illinois, Minnesota, Nebraska, Pennsylvania, Tennessee, Wisconsin, Michigan, Oregon, Massachusetts, South Carolina, and Ohio. In 7 of these states—Pennsylvania, Tennessee, Connecticut, South Carolina, Massachusetts, Wisconsin, and Ohio—the local self-help clearinghouse had no listings for self-help groups for older women. An unsuccessful attempt was made to contact self-help clearinghouses in an additional 3 states, Vermont, New Hampshire, and Georgia. According to the National Self-Help Clearinghouse, a number of self-help clearinghouses located around the country have closed down in recent years as a result of insufficient funding.

National Agencies. In addition to the clearinghouses mentioned above, the following national agencies were contacted for information regarding self-help support groups for older women: American Association of Retired Persons' Women's Initiative, National Organization of Area Agencies on Aging, the National Older Women's League, and the Women's Self-Help Clearinghouse.

The names and locations of those self-help groups and their sponsoring agencies (where appropriate) included in the national survey are listed below.

PARTICIPATING SELF-HELP GROUPS IN THE NATIONAL SURVEY

Name of Group	Name of Sponsoring Agency	Location
Client Support Group	Senior Health and Peer Counseling Center	Santa Monica, CA
Support Unlimited	Suncoast Center for Community Mental Health, Senior Support Services Department	St. Petersburg, FL
Support Group for Older Women	North Shore Senior Center	Northfield, IL
Mid-Life Support Group	Women's Health Resources	Chicago, IL
Peer Support Program	Jackson County Department on Aging	Jackson, MI
A Support Group for Women over 55	Chrysalis Center for Women	Minneapolis, MN
Alone Not Alone	Grace Lutheran Church	Lincoln, NE
Women Over Fifty Living Alone	National Council of Jewish Women, Center for Women, Project GRO	Livingston, NJ
Adjusting to Later Life Changes	Kennedy Gerontology Center	Stratford, NJ
Women Talk		Scarsdale, NY
Women in Search of a More Positive Sense of Self		Larchmont, NY
Prime Pathways		Houston, TX

Interviews

Telephone interviews were conducted with 14 experts associated with 12 groups in nine states. Each interview lasted approximately 30–45 minutes. Interviewees were support group coordinators and lay and professional facilitators of support groups for older women. Interviews were conducted with the assistance of a semistructured, open-ended survey questionnaire developed especially for this study that explores such topics as the basic philosophy of the self-help program; the central characteristics of group participants; the function and responsibility of group facilitators and leaders; the content of self-help group discussions; the level of organizational resources required for program delivery; the extent to which self-help groups increase older women's ability to cope with loneliness, stress, depression and loss; and the extent to which these groups serve as informal support networks for their members.

FINDINGS FROM THE NATIONAL SURVEY

Purpose of the Program

All 12 programs provide an opportunity for older adults to support one another. Many of the programs make a special effort to distinguish these peer support groups from therapy groups. According to the group facilitator, the goal of support groups at the Senior Health and Peer Counseling Center is to assist older people in discovering how they can make each moment count. As a group leader, she tries to help people understand that their lives can be easily as exciting and productive today as they were forty years ago. Peer counseling is an integral part of this process because (a) older people may be more likely to speak with their peers than with professional counselors and (b) peer counselors serve as role models for their clients.

The goal of the Peer Support Program at the Jackson County Department on Aging is to help people experiencing stress and loneliness in coping with difficult situations, adjusting to major life changes, and making and establishing new friendships. Like the Senior Health and Peer Counseling Center, the Jackson County program believes that the success of the program is seniors helping seniors by listening, giving support, making referrals, and helping other elders to make their own decisions.

The peer support groups offered by Project GRO of the National Council of Jewish Women's Center for Women provides older women with an opportunity to meet others in similar life circumstances who are experiencing normal, but sometimes frustrating or confusing life situations. The coordinator of this program explains that Project GRO groups, aptly named Women Over Fifty Living Alone, differ from therapy groups because the former emphasize mutual support, sharing of concerns, idea exchange, and the development of networks.

The goal of Prime Pathways is to educate women and to help them bond with one another. Women Talk describes its purpose as helping women meet new women. The Sun Coast Center for Community Mental Health's Support Unlimited groups encourage social interaction with older adults and an opportunity for problem solving.

The Kennedy Gerontology Center's Adjusting to Later Life Changes group challenges older adults to join a discussion support group in order to enhance their coping skills, accept life changes, meet new people, and share their experiences with others.

Many of the support groups exist within the broader context of health, mental health, and senior or women's centers. The groups located at these institutions further the missions of these larger institutions. For example, the mission of Chrysalis Center for Women is to empower older women individually and collectively by encouraging personal change and by initiating social change. This empowerment goal is a consistent one for several programs, including the SOWN program. The Senior Health and Peer Counseling Center is dedicated to enhancing the quality of life of older adults through the improvement of their mental and physical health. The goal of Suncoast Center for Community Mental Health is to enhance the overall quality of life of their senior clients and assure independent living for them as long as possible.

CHARACTERISTICS OF THE WOMEN SERVED

Gender

Seven of the 12 groups studied serve women only. Three of these groups are sponsored by women's programs and women's centers that focus on women's health and psychosocial well-being. The 5 groups that welcome men have few in attendance. Some group leaders of mixed groups have identified differences in the needs of men and women within their groups.

Age

Most programs define an age parameter that serves as a qualification of group membership. These age parameters vary: 45–60 years (predominantly 47–50 years); 45 years and older (average age is 55 years); 50–60 years; 50 years and over (average age is early 60s); 55–70 years (predominantly 58–64 years); 55–75 years; 55–80 years; 55 years and older (with members in their 50s, 60s, and 70s); 60–85 years (average age is 70 years); 60 years and older (most members in their 70s and 80s); and 70 years and older (approximately half in their 80s). Some groups have participants in their 90s.

The older group participants in one group have asked that a separate group be created for women 80 years and older to reflect the different needs of the "younger" and "older" women. Project GRO separates women in the Recently Separated and Widows groups into older and younger categories.

Race

Eight of the groups currently consist of Whites only. The remaining four groups serve a primarily White clientele. One of these groups includes one African American and several Mexican American group members. Another includes African Americans and Latinos. Yet another group includes African Americans and Asian Americans. Although Latinos are not currently participating in the groups at Senior

Health and Peer Counseling Center, the individual peer counseling program includes a Latino component.

Many facilitators report that their programs primarily serve White women because the areas in which the groups are located are overwhelmingly populated by Whites.

Economic Status

Most of the participants in the self-help support groups studied were working or middle class. Typically, group members were neither very wealthy nor indigent. Two programs were composed of upper-middle-class women. In Texas, participants in Prime Pathways are often women who have recently experienced a decline in their income as a result of the sluggish economy. Many of the groups had as one of their ongoing topics helping older women to cope with their diminished economic means.

Marital Status

Although some women are married during the time of their association with group self-help, many of the participants are widowed or divorced. For a number of these women, the challenges associated with managing alone for the first time in their lives are just beginning to be confronted when they join a support group. For these women, the group can represent an important forum in which to deal with issues surrounding the loss of a spouse. The groups encourage women to share their difficulties with other women experiencing similar problems. The groups, therefore, often discuss the impact of widowhood or divorce on their members, including such matters as managing financially, living alone, dealing with loneliness, meeting other men, and discovering alternative sources and means by which to express feelings of love and intimacy.

GROUP STRATEGIES AND METHODS

Recruitment

As was discussed earlier in the case of SOWN (chapter 6), the most popular form of recruitment is personalized outreach and word of mouth. Often, however, personalized, face-to-face strategies of outreach are combined with other approaches to recruitment, including public service announcements, given that the latter can be carried out with little or no costs in terms of time and money accruing to the group. One group produced 3-minute and 10-minute public service announcements that were aired on local radio stations. Most groups are listed with their local self-help clearinghouse or information and referral service. The programs that are affiliated with larger institutions receive assistance with recruitment from their parent agencies. For example, one group is sponsored by a hospital that sends flyers to the 16,000 members of its senior program. Other institutions send newsletters to their members and to psychologists and private practitioners in the community. Another group meets at a senior citizen center that publicizes the group in its bulletin.

One group sends brochures to women's centers, adult children of alcoholics groups, and psychologists. Another group places flyers in senior citizen high rises and bookstores. Some groups have received special media attention. For example, the Senior Health and Peer Counseling Center appeared on the television show "20/20" and was recognized nationally and locally for being chosen as one of former President Bush's "Thousand Points of Light." Another program provides training sessions to ministerial and other interested groups. A number of programs receive referrals from doctors, mental health professionals, and clergy in their communities. One program, located in a church, recruits through the church bulletin. Another advertises its program at local health fairs.

At least one group coordinator has adapted her outreach strategy to reflect her suspicion that women will be reluctant to join a group that emphasizes aging. The cover of this group's brochure announces that the group is "a life affirming support group for bolder, not older women."

Screening

Most programs have some form of procedure for screening prospective group members on criteria that include but are not limited to the age parameters illustrated above. At the Senior Health and Peer Counseling Center, prospective group members are screened carefully: An intake interview is conducted at the center, followed by a phone or face-to-face interview with a facilitator. Prospective members of the Suncoast Center for Community Mental Health's Support Unlimited group receive 1–3 months of individual counseling before they are referred to a group. Group members are then hand picked and must have resolved their most serious issues with a therapist before entering a group. Widowed individuals are screened carefully and must be beyond heavy grief before they are able to join. Clients of the Peer Support program at the Jackson County Department on Aging must meet the following criteria: She or he is not under treatment elsewhere (a number of clients would "group hop"), she or he is experiencing stress due to social and or physical problems, and she or he is lonely or depressed because of social and or physical problems. Clients with serious mental health problems, such as suicidal tendencies, are screened out of the group. Finally, clients must agree to abide by stringent confidentiality standards in order to join a group. At Women's Health Resources, prospective group members are screened on the phone; few are discouraged from attending as a result of this initial interview. After attending a few group sessions, a new member who joins Women in Search of a More Positive Sense of Self decides together with established members of the group whether or not she should be accepted into the group. Women Talk implemented a telephone screening procedure after a severely depressed and heavily medicated woman attended one of their sessions.

Logistics of Group Meetings

Most groups meet at the site of the sponsoring institutions, including a church, a women's health center, a gerontology center, a mental health center, senior centers, and women's centers. Three groups meet at the homes of group members. Two groups meet at nursing homes.

Five of the groups meet weekly, three meet monthly, three meet twice a month, and one met weekly for the first few years and now meets twice a month. Six of the groups meet during the day, and three meet in the evening. Groups meet for varying lengths of time, many for 1–1.5 hours (as is the case for SOWN groups). When a group is composed of particularly healthy and somewhat younger older adults, they may hold meetings lasting as long as 2 or 3 hours. Groups meeting for these longer periods of time usually include time required for the guest speaker presentations and refreshment breaks in calculating the length of the overall session.

Duration of Group

All the groups with the exception of four meet on an ongoing basis, and many have been meeting together for years. One Client Support Group at the Senior Health and Peer Counseling Center has been meeting together for 5 years. The peer support group program at Senior Health and Peer Counseling Center has been in existence for more than 15 years. Members of Women in Search of a More Positive Sense of Self have been meeting together for more than 3 years, and a core group of five or six women have been meeting together at Chrysalis Center for Women for more than 2 years. Suncoast Center for Community Mental Health's Support Unlimited group has been meeting for 13 years, though most of the original members no longer attend. Women Talk, Prime Pathways, and Adjusting to Later Life Changes have all been in existence for over a year.

Of the groups that meet on a time-limited basis, one meets for 11 sessions. The other three groups offer members the opportunity to continue to meet after the group officially ends. Project GRO groups meet with a professional facilitator for 8 weeks, after which the participants are encouraged to meet on their own. At Women's Health Resources, group participants are asked to make a 3-month commitment. Groups often continue to meet after this time. Chrysalis Center for Women groups meet for 8 weeks, break for a week, and then begin a new 8-week cycle. Many women continue to attend more than one 8-week group, although Chrysalis encourages women to work through their issues and then find other channels of support. Chrysalis reports that women attending their older women's support group tend to want to continue with the group more than do women in other support groups offered by Chrysalis. The facilitator believes this is because older women have weaker support systems.

Size of Group and Enrollment

Group size ranges from 6 to 25 members, with an average of 10 or 11. The facilitator of Adjusting to Later Life Changes reports that she has difficulty maintaining strong group process because her group numbers 20 members. Most facilitators express the view that a smaller group, numbering around 10 people, better enables group members to share and learn. In one group, sessions are canceled if fewer than 3 people attend.

Groups that meet on an ongoing basis welcome new members. Groups that are time-limited usually close enrollment after the first few sessions.

FUNCTIONS AND RESPONSIBILITIES OF GROUP LEADERS

Five groups are professionally facilitated, five are peer facilitated, one is facilitated by both a professional facilitator and a peer facilitator, and one group does not arrange for any facilitation at meetings. Four of the groups that use some form of peer facilitation provide extensive training for their peer counselors. In the other, peer facilitators are not trained and leadership responsibility rotates.

Role of Facilitator

Both professional and peer facilitators of self-help support groups for older women assume responsibility for the following tasks:

- facilitating group discussion
- providing information and referrals
- establishing group ground rules
- presenting options
- paying attention to group process, including (a) making sure that no one dominates the discussion, (b) encouraging all group members to participate in discussions and problem solving, (c) monitoring the feelings of individual participants, and (d) facilitating group bonding

Most facilitators do not enter the group with a fixed agenda, but many are prepared with exercises that will facilitate discussion. Prime Pathways is the only group with a structured format. The coordinator talks for 10 minutes at the beginning of each session. Her presentation is followed by a speaker, and then the group breaks into smaller groups for discussion. The facilitator at North Shore Senior Center, who leads two groups, reports that she makes more presentations in the group composed of women who are relatively older.

Challenges Faced by Facilitators

Facilitators report that one of the major challenges is trying to meet the needs of individual group members without sacrificing the needs of the entire group. In one group, a severely depressed woman was negatively influencing group process, causing other group members to withdraw or leave. The facilitator of this group reports that many group members are depressed. Consequently, her role sometimes fluctuates between that of facilitator and that of counselor or therapist.

A number of facilitators report that it is common for one or two women to talk excessively and have difficulty relating to the group as a whole. The greatest challenge for these facilitators is to control these people and to encourage all group members to participate. Another facilitator reports that maintaining a positive atmosphere is difficult in her group, where members tend to be pessimistic. Furthermore, as she is a younger woman, some group members remind her of the generation gap. A few facilitators would like group members to take greater responsibility for the group, thus diminishing the facilitator's influence. A facilitator whose group meets in a nursing home reports that nonmembers sometime disturb the group by poking their heads in to determine who is there on a given day. This facilitator decided to lock the door once the group begins. In one group, some group members verbally attacked other members and accused them of being dirty and of not belonging. One person accused another of not being a good Christian. Another facilitator reports that her group members tend to avoid exploration of their feelings.

PEER FACILITATION PROGRAMS AND TRAINING

Four programs—Senior Health and Peer Counseling Center, National Counsel of Jewish Women's Project GRO, Chrysalis Center for Women, and Peer Support Program of Jackson County, Michigan—offer training programs for peer facilitators. Two of the training programs are designed to assist peer counselors in a variety of settings. For example, among the many groups Project GRO offers are groups for divorced women, single mothers, widows, and mothers with children under 5. Chrysalis offers many groups, including groups for women in their middle years, lesbians, single mothers, and compulsive eaters. The peer training for group leaders at the Senior Health and Peer Counseling Center is preceded by an extensive training for peer counselors working with individual clients.

At Project GRO, peer facilitators receive 9 weeks of training. Topics include the following: what is peer support, how to run a peer support group, group process, reflective listening techniques, and how to deal with difficult group members. Trainees participate in role plays that allow them to practice their skills. Peer facilitators speak on a weekly basis with a professional supervisor and meet with her once during the 8-week session. Six in-service training workshops are offered to peer facilitators annually, of which they must attend three in order to remain active. Peer trainers range in age from their late 20s to their 70s.

At the Senior Health and Peer Counseling Center, group leaders are recruited from the ranks of individual peer counselors, who must complete a 12-week, 24-session training program. Training sessions include the following topics:

- psychology of aging
- ABCs of counseling
- communication is a process
- group process
- counseling interventions
- death and dying, grief and loss
- depression, suicide, and loneliness
- enhancing your lifestyle
- integrating the physical and emotional
- stress reduction
- taking care of yourself in the counseling situation
- new directions for seniors
- case management and family systems
- community resources and record keeping
- getting started with clients
- endings create beginnings

A 250-page training manual accompanies the one-on-one peer counseling training program. The manual, which includes a week-by-week guide to the training sessions, also includes information about developing and administering a peer counseling program and recruiting and selecting trainees.

Peer counselors who go on to become group leaders receive additional training. The Senior Health and Peer Counseling Center credits the low attrition it experiences with peer counselors to a careful trainee selection process that includes a written application, face-to-face interview, and small group interviews and maintaining a firm commitment of 8 hours per week for 1 year, careful selection of the trainer or supervisor, formal supervision, and the opportunity counselors receive for continuing education. Group leaders receive weekly supervision while their groups meet.

The Peer Support Program at Jackson County Department on Aging provides a 20-hour training for peer listeners. The training covers the following topics:

- the aging process, including myths and realities
- physiology of aging
- behavioral changes
- sensory changes and mental changes
- communication skills
- listening skills
- problem solving
- stress
- isolation
- loss associated with death, job, divorce, surgery, or accident of friends or family members
- loneliness
- depression
- physical ailments and major illnesses
- social or physical family problems including loss of home, friends, and independence
- referrals

An 80-page manual accompanies the training and includes material for the 20-hour training as well as a description of the program, its funding, and recruitment of clients and volunteers. Peer listeners facilitate group meetings with the assistance of the Peer Support Program director.

Prospective peer listeners at Peer Support Program are screened carefully; they are interviewed and asked to respond to a series of statements most likely made by clients. Examples are "My husband died and left me all alone," "I need to wear oxygen all the time now and I don't want to go out in public," "The doctor said I shouldn't drive my car anymore," and "My daughter says my hair looks awful and I should dye it. I would look better. I like it this way. Why should she say such a hateful thing?" A peer support volunteer should be someone who is

- a good listener
- an understanding person
- a friendly person

- one who likes to work with senior citizens
- one who can give encouragement
- one who can give praise
- a knowledgeable person
- one who will allow the senior citizen to make his or her own decisions
- one who can keep information confidential

The peer volunteer also receives an exit interview, at which time she is asked to assess the overall quality of her experience with the group. Included in the interview are questions that encourage the volunteer to evaluate the strengths and weaknesses of the group with which she was associated, her own capacities as a peer facilitator, and the extent to which the Peer Support Program met her needs during the course of her volunteer experience.

Whereas the Peer Support Program provides volunteer facilitators with 20 hours of training, Chrysalis Center for Women peer counselors receive a 60-hour training that includes the following material:

- overview of Chrysalis
- how to give feedback
- explanation of the difference between support groups and therapy
- role playing
- gay and lesbian issues
- abuse issues
- mental health issues
- personal limitations of facilitators
- structuring a meeting, including openings and closings
- paperwork
- legal issues
- AIDS
- safe sex
- suicide
- domestic abuse
- handling critical incidents, such as panic attacks
- what is supportive and what is not supportive
- self-disclosure
- communication skills such as conflict resolution and how to focus questions
- active listening
- how to deal with problem group members
- self-awareness
- making referrals
- group process
- leadership qualities
- racial issues
- grief issues

Each peer counselor must have participated in some type of peer support group before she can become a group leader. Peer counselors work in pairs. A supervisor comes in once to observe the session. In-service training occurs year round. Peer counselors for the older women's group must be 55 or over.

CONTENT OF SELF-HELP GROUP SESSIONS

As was seen with the SOWN program, identifying and then developing session content topics is an aspect of group facilitation where help is needed. As a result, the support group programs surveyed commonly provide both peer and staff facilitators with extensive examples of topics for presentation. The listing of topics boxed below (not in order of popularity) are often discussed in meetings of the support groups for older women that were surveyed. They have been organized according to common themes. Similarities can be seen between this topical listing and session topics identified during the course of the SOWN research (see Table 5-2).

COMMON TOPICS DISCUSSED IN SUPPORT GROUPS FOR OLDER WOMEN

Topics Addressing Personal Development Issues
- loneliness
- mortality
- how to make each moment count
- self-esteem
- future fears and desires
- how members see themselves in 5 years
- life transitions
- ageism
- how to maintain independence
- health issues, including fear of illness, learning to live with chronic illness, and advance directives
- physical changes, including vision, hearing, and mobility
- energy level changes
- lack of mobility
- isolation
- weight gain

Topics Addressing Daily Life Issues
- practical issues such as house maintenance, car mechanics, and traveling alone
- financial matters and financial management
- work
- loss of job
- retirement
- legal issues, including moving to smaller quarters, learning to live alone, and living with relatives

Topics Addressing Family and Social Relationships
- companionship
- friendship
- children
- grandchildren
- sexuality and relationships
- social issues
- caregiving
- desertion by families
- husbands at home
- death of friends

The generic listing of topics presented in the box are drawn on in a variety of ways by different group programs. In addition, variations on the topical themes can be identified. For example, the coordinator of Prime Pathways plans to discuss some of the following topics in group meetings: accepting losses, problems with grown children, shortage of quality men, overcoming resentments, lower standard of living, and compulsions or addictions.

In another group, the facilitator presents a list of topics from which members choose what they would like to discuss. The facilitator of another group asks if anybody would like to process something from last group, or she may bring in an exercise that pertains to the preceding week's discussion. This facilitator does reminiscence therapy with her group; she asks group members to bring in six pictures and share memories. She also introduces stress management, relaxation, and positive-thinking exercises. Another facilitator asks her group to write their autobiographies. Women who attend Prime Pathways meetings have been asked to list 12 things that give them pleasure, 12 ways they could make money, and 12 reasons they deserve to be successful. Speakers have addressed this group on such topics as growing older more beautifully, inner and outer image, inner child, gynecology, the potent woman, and self-defense. The facilitator of Prime Pathways leads guided meditations and uses written exercises. One group, located at a women's health center, intended to talk about women's health issues such as menopause. Instead, the group tends to discuss relationship issues and sexuality.

ESTABLISHING GROUP PROCEDURES

Many groups establish group ground rules. For example, in one group, members are asked to agree to the following rules: Respect privacy, give everyone an opportunity to talk, don't be judgmental, and relate to one person and one topic at a time. In the Jackson County Peer Support Program, confidentiality is considered the most important rule that all members must agree to before the group can begin its work.

In another program, group members are asked to establish goals at the first session. It is considered critical that the goal formulation process be one in which there is broad-scale involvement of all members. The sharing of responsibility for developing goals better ensures that all members of the group will have ownership of them and a sense of responsibility for working toward their realization. These goals are reviewed midway through the training. Common goals of older adult self-help support groups include working toward individual and group empowerment, the provision and receipt of peer support, and the establishment of a sense of community among members.

The majority of facilitators do not come in with fixed agendas. However, many prepare an opening exercise for the group. For example, members may be asked to share how they are feeling at the beginning of each session. At Chrysalis, the facilitator sometimes asks members to talk about the most difficult thing that occurred in the past week or may present members with a "feelings chart" from which they are asked to identify a feeling that describes their current emotional state. This facilitator often begins sessions by reading the Chrysalis philosophy, which states that the group serves as a safe place, where each woman discovers her own answers and her own timing, and that each woman is considered a whole woman at the outset. Then, she asks each group member to talk about which part of the Chrysalis philosophy makes most sense to her right now. Following this, group members are asked if they want time during that session; session time is then divided by the number of people who want to speak. No one may interrupt while another person is sharing, and a few minutes are saved at the end of each person's time for feedback from the group.

Gender and Content

Facilitators report that men and women share similar concerns. One facilitator reports that sexuality is a particularly significant issue for the men in her group. Men are threatened by their impotence and tend to blame their wives and partners for their feelings of sexual inadequacy. The facilitator believes that the presence of women in the group is helpful. Another facilitator reports that the men and women in her group sometimes have different interests and hobbies, which can result in lack of interest in what the other is saying.

Age and Content

The North Shore Senior Center runs two peer support groups for older women. One of them meets in a nursing home and is composed of women in their 70s and 80s. Issues discussed in this group are somewhat different than issues discussed in the other group, whose average age is lower. For example, the group that meets in the nursing home talks more about health and financial issues as members have more health and financial problems. Project GRO's Recently Separated and Widows groups are divided into younger and older categories. The younger women more often discuss dating and children.

Organizational Resources and Funding

Some of the peer support programs studied have large budgets, others have no budgets at all. Six employ volunteers as group leaders. The Senior Health and Peer Counseling Center has a $1.5 million budget, of which 31% is government funding, including a grant from the city of Santa Monica. Almost half the funding comes from contributions, endowments, and foundation grants. Group members are not charged, but are asked to make a contribution. The peer support groups at the Sun Coast Center for Community Mental Health are also free of charge, but participants are urged to contribute what they can. This program receives funding under the Older Americans Act. Most funds for the support groups at Project GRO come from a displaced homemakers grant from the state of New Jersey. Participants in the 8-week sessions are charged a fee of $35, which may be waived. The support groups at the Kennedy Gerontology Center receive funding from the William Penn Foundation, New Jersey higher education grants, and the Robert Wood Johnson Foundation. The groups also receive some hospital support. There is no fee for the peer support group. Prime Pathways receives no funding; the facilitator offers her house and coffee for free. Participants are charged $8 per session. Women Talk and Women in Search of a More Positive Sense of Self are unfunded and meet in the participants' homes. Individuals participate without cost. Alone Not Alone receives minimal financial support from the church at which it is housed. Chrysalis receives support from United Way, foundations, and donations, and it charges fees for services. Participants, but not facilitators, are charged up to $7 per session. Jackson County Department on Aging receives a grant from the Area Agency on Aging in Michigan. The grant has been renewed for the fifth time.

Effectiveness of Self-Help Support Groups

All program experts interviewed for this study report that their groups are very successful. They point to the longevity of the groups and the stable attendance as proof that the service is needed and valued by the women who participate. Facilitators report that older women enter the group feeling isolated and having weak support systems. A peer support group provides the older person with an opportunity to meet people and discuss personal issues in a friendly, nonjudgmental environment. A new stage in life brings on new feelings. Peer support groups are forums where older adults can process these feelings. The groups create a "safe space" where people who share similar perspectives on life can talk about their fears, concerns, and expectations associated with growing older in our society.

The facilitator of Adjusting to Later Life Changes reports that women in her group increase their self esteem and self worth by talking with their peers about issues of common concern. Group members have an appreciation of what their peers have been through and a respect for the past. Project GRO reports a 96% satisfaction rate from participant evaluation forms. The facilitator of Sun Coast Center for Community Mental Health groups believes they are effective because older people are able to relate to others who have experienced similar problems, learn from one another, share experiences, and gain deeper insight into their personal life circumstances. The facilitator at Alone Not Alone reports that years ago, when such groups did not exist, she used to take long drives in her car to relieve her feelings. Many group leaders stress the importance of the nonjudgmental feedback that group participants receive from one another. Participants who complete Chrysalis's evaluation forms report that they are more assertive, better able to take care of themselves, and better able to release unrealistic expectations of themselves. Social workers at the nursing home where one group operates report that group members are more active in other activities, easier to get along with, and more assertive. One facilitator reports that group members become better listeners and problem solvers as the group progresses. The Jackson County Peer Support Program assists people who have been abandoned by the system. The facilitator reports that one woman was totally withdrawn and refused to walk before she joined a group. Since joining the group, the woman is significantly less withdrawn and has begun to walk. This facilitator also reports that people who have dementia sometimes achieve heightened levels of coherency within the group.

In an article appearing in the city newspaper, a woman who participates in the Senior Health and Peer Counseling Center program reported that when she entered the peer-counseling program for the newly widowed, she discovered that depression, loneliness, and a feeling of loss of productivity could be shared by others. That proved to be an important first step toward recovering her positive self-image. One 70-year-old woman who participates in a group at the Senior Health and Peer Counseling Center maintains that as one gets older, you discover you have fewer people to hug. She is able to hug people in her group. The group is family to her.

Self-Help Groups as Informal Support Networks

In many programs, participants are discouraged from meeting together outside of the group session. Facilitators in these groups believe that socializing outside of group can be destructive to the group process. For example, if two members develop a friendship that turns sour, one or both may decide to leave the group. One facilitator discourages socializing outside of the group because she believes that group members may not be looking for this level of intensity or involvement with other group members. Another facilitator began to discourage extragroup interaction because fights and gossip about group members resulted.

Other group leaders encourage participants to network outside of the group. Phone numbers are exchanged. Networking among group members may include exchanging information about places to live, churches, job networking, entrepreneurship, and elder day care. One facilitator serves coffee and cookies before her group begins and encourages the group to network informally before she arrives. Although this facilitator does not encourage socializing outside of the group as much as she once did, she sometimes will suggest that two people who are members of the same group consider meeting with each other outside of group sessions. The group that meets at Sun Coast Center is encouraged to participate in center activities, including birthday parties and dances. At Women's Health Resources, group members make plans to participate in activities together. At Women Talk, many group members are friends and are in close contact with one another outside of the group. At Prime Pathways, the facilitator successfully encourages participants to go out to Saturday lunch or to the movies. This facilitator believes that the group will be more cohesive if members socialize outside of the group. Participants in another group often arrive 45 minutes early and stay for a reduced-cost lunch at the hospital cafeteria.

If money were not an issue, some groups would expand to increase the number of older women they could reach. One facilitator would buy state-of-the-art equipment and would order films that would help stimulate conversations. Unfortunately, money is always an issue for support groups, necessarily influencing the scope and breadth of programming that can be offered the membership.

CONCLUSION

Although the availability of self-help support groups for older women remains at a premium throughout the United States, there are excellent examples of group initiatives that are serving as prototypes of this category of service intervention. Many of these groups have been highlighted in this chapter. These groups are pioneers in self-help programming. Many lessons can be learned from the guidelines by which they operate and the strategies they use to deal with issues related to the dynamics of group function. Taken in combination with the experience of SOWN, the practice principles driving these programs should prove very informative to those considering the development of self-help groups for older women in local communities without existing programmatic resources of this type.

9

Issues and Practice Principles Arising from an Archetypal Self-Help Group

This chapter presents an extended case study of an archetypal self-help support group for older women. It highlights a variety of program organization and operation issues that may arise at different points in the life of the group. The strategy of moving into and out of the vignette in order to present professional responses, principles, and commentary is used. The issues focused on are generalized from information culled throughout the course of the research.

INSTIGATING FACTORS IN GROUP FORMATION

As long-time members of the same urban congregation, Mrs. Lindsey and Ms. Nichols often socialized outside of church. Over the years, through periods of illness, family crises, and even widowhood, the two were always available to support each other. They shared happy times as well, attending each other's family functions and participating in a variety of recreational activities together. As the women grew older, both entering their 70s, they found there were times when one was not able to help the other in a time of need. Shortly after Ms. Nichols returned home from a hospitalization for intestinal surgery, Mrs. Lindsey's husband died unexpectedly, preventing either one from fully assisting the other with a major life event. Such situations led the friends to discuss the value of their relationship and concerns regarding the availability of ongoing mutual support as they faced the issues of aging and old age. On hearing of their concerns, Mrs. Lindsey's daughter, a former member of a 12-step program, suggested that they engage a few more women for a "women's group." The two jumped at the idea, not fully recognizing the amount of effort that would be required.

Professionals and lay persons alike must be aware of the planning necessary for establishing a self-help support group. Although the planning process is not particularly complex or extensive, the absence of proper preparation frequently results in an unsuccessful group or one that does not altogether get off the ground. The less bureaucratic, informal structure of most support organizations may inaccurately convey a message to the contrary.

Careful consideration must be given to several factors to ensure successful implementation. Critical components in the planning process include, but are not limited to, the following: (a) conducting a needs assessment, (b) identifying a sponsor or securing funding, (c) selecting a meeting site, (d) choosing and preparing a facilitator, (e) developing a marketing plan, (f) conducting outreach, (g) screening potential members, and (h) preparing session topics.

Established self-help groups are usually pleased to provide assistance to fledgling organizations by providing guidance and, in certain cases, materials. Manuals are available as well to help structure the support group planning process.

THE LOGISTICS OF GROUP DEVELOPMENT

Ms. Nichols and Mrs. Lindsey went from being excited about their venture to feeling overwhelmed at the prospect of handling the requisite logistics and finally to being dedicated to making their vision a reality. With significant assistance from Mrs. Lindsey's daughter, they made a list of everything that had to be done.

First, they decided that their church would be an ideal location for group meetings. It was located in a central and safe part of the city, was within a block of a bus stop, and was just four blocks from an apartment building for retirees. They approached their minister to request the use of a classroom for 1 hour per week, ideally a weekday afternoon, which was the preferred time for social and recreational activities among their peers. The classrooms and handicapped-accessible bathrooms were all on the main floor, which would allow easy access by those with difficulty ambulating or the wheelchair bound. Additionally, the room afforded appropriate privacy for the women to discuss personal issues comfortably. The minister inquired whether the women intended the group to be an activity sponsored by the church or, rather, a community activity that was simply located at the church. After careful consideration, the women opted for the latter as they agreed that they would seek members from the larger community with the goal of attracting a more diverse population. Their request for space was approved for Wednesday afternoons from 3:00 to 4:00 p.m. with the exception of holidays and special church events.

The next step was planning and conducting outreach. This process raised several issues:

1. In what ways would they limit membership? Would men be absolutely excluded? Would they set an unwavering age limit?
2. Should they target the more active and well elderly exclusively or include those who might be slightly infirm or impaired?
3. How many members would be optimal? What would they do about those wanting to join after they reached capacity? Would there be a "waiting list?"
4. Would there be a limited number of sessions or would the group be ongoing? At what point, if any, would new members be invited to join?
5. To what extent should they define the group's goals and identify topics for discussion before getting input from members?
6. What methods of outreach would be most effective?
7. Who would pay for outreach efforts?
8. How could they attract a diverse population of older women, particularly with regard to socioeconomic status and ethnic or racial minority status?

9. What address or phone number would be placed on a flyer for those wanting information or choosing to join?

It was clear that such questions had to be answered before proceeding.

Although support groups are supposed to be the creation of their members, certain decisions and parameters must be set in advance to draw participants. Except in cases where an existing group of persons jointly decide to form a mutual aid organization, there will be one or a few planners who must make decisions on the basis of limited knowledge of potential members' preferences. A conscientious needs assessment and familiarity with the target market are key tools for meaningful planning. Potential group members' decisions to join or not join a support organization will be heavily influenced by the purpose and structure defined by planners. However, it is important to note that once a group is in operation, members should be given the opportunity to discuss and revise many facets of what is now their own forum.

OUTREACH AND MARKETING STRATEGIES

Only those decisions that had to be made prior to the group's commencement were addressed by Mrs. Lindsey and Ms. Nichols. The remainder, they concurred, would ultimately be presented to the group for discussion and a vote.

Outreach materials invited "women seniors" without specifying an age limitation. It was adequate, they felt, to attract women, regardless of chronological age, who identified with the senior citizen population. No mention was made of physical or mental condition. Registration would be limited to 15 participants, with the remainder of applicants (should there be any) placed on a waiting list. Those on the waiting list would be invited to join in the order they originally presented themselves to fill vacancies created by anyone who left the group. Additionally, at the end of 12 weeks, those on the waiting list would be given an opportunity to rotate into the group through a process to be determined by the original group. Both Ms. Nichols and Mrs. Lindsey secretly hoped for no waiting list, as the logistics of its management seemed complicated and potentially a source of conflict among participants who might not want to rotate out.

The types and extent of outreach were limited by financial constraints. The two women now realized that by declining an association with the church, they were concurrently cutting off a significant source of financial and in-kind support. Marketing was therefore limited to flyers distributed to a few local churches and synagogues, a neighborhood senior citizen center, the public library, and the nearby apartment complex for elderly people. Several others were posted in area groceries, drug stores, and other businesses frequented by the elderly. A deliberate attempt was made to reach out to neighboring areas with different demographic compositions with the goal of attracting minority women and those of a variety of socioeconomic classes. The costs incurred for copying were absorbed by the "founding partners," as they ultimately called themselves.

Ms. Nichols volunteered to place her phone number, although not her name, on the outreach materials. She already had an answering machine and willingly changed the recording.

Choosing to have a parent organization or, instead, opting to establish a self-help group without a formal affiliation can have a significant impact on a developing mutual support group. Developing a program as an offering of an organization such as a religious institution, senior center, or retirement community has several benefits, including a source of funding, a guaranteed meeting location, and the credibility of a known entity. Additionally, under the auspices of a larger enterprise, the group will likely be the recipient of in-kind benefits such as printing and copying, telephone use for both making and receiving calls, support staff effort, meeting refreshments, and inclusion in marketing materials such as newsletters.

The downside to such an affiliation is a loss of some or all autonomy in decision making. Also, the image or stereotype of a parent organization might discourage certain potential participants who feel that they do not fit in. For example, an affiliation with a church or synagogue might negatively influence those of another faith. Similarly, a group held in a senior citizens' center might want to attract those who are not center members, yet some candidates for the self-help program might hesitate to join because they do not see themselves as the "senior center type."

GROUP FACILITATION

Although the group would ultimately have input into the selection of a facilitator, Mrs. Lindsey offered to fulfill the role until an alternative was selected or to serve indefinitely, should the group so choose. Her years as a substitute teacher, she claimed, prepared her well for speaking in front of a group and moderating gatherings. She additionally had the necessary free time available to plan for each week's session. Her daughter was helpful in providing a thorough description of the facilitator role, based on her own experiences as a support group participant. Ms. Nichols was designated as the backup facilitator in the event that Mrs. Lindsey were unavailable, a job the more introverted woman accepted with trepidation.

A facilitator can make or break a self-help support group, making the selection of a qualified leader a critical one. A mistake some groups make is choosing the most popular member of the group as the facilitator rather than looking more closely for the requisite qualities and skills.

Ideally, the facilitator should be an empathetic listener and have the ability to rephrase members' comments in a way that is meaningful to others. She should be outwardly nonjudgmental and help other participants appreciate differences as well. As appropriate, she should be able to recognize and highlight commonalties to diffuse rising tensions. Because the facilitator is also looked up to as a role model, it is imperative that she be able to handle her own difficult issues and not shy away from topics or conflicts. And she should be secure enough to empower others without feeling threatened herself, as this is a key goal of self-help support groups. Finally, the group leader has to be willing and able to handle the administrative tasks that are an inevitable part of the position. These include preparing each week's session plan, maintaining the attendance records, and, in some cases, handling the logistics related to the meeting location and refreshments.

THE DEVELOPMENT OF GROUND RULES

Fortunately for Ms. Nichols and Mrs. Lindsey, they received calls of inquiry from 13 older women and, by the week prior to the first meeting, had an enrollment of 9 in addition to themselves.

To help them plan some preliminary discussion topics, the organizers asked those enrolled a few questions about themselves. These conversations were useful not only to obtain information on potential participants, but also to confirm that each one had the mental and verbal ability to contribute to a self-help support group. All but one of the women were over 60 years of age. The remaining participant was 56 and the only member who was still in the workforce, albeit on a very part-time basis. Four were married and living with a spouse, whereas the others were either widowed or unmarried. All reported themselves to be in at least fair health. Most described themselves as being among the "well elderly." One member, due to difficulties ambulating, would be accompanied by an aide who would wait outside of the classroom during meeting time. The women did not ask questions regarding financial or minority status for fear that their motives in doing so would be misinterpreted.

Ground rules are another absolute necessity for the initial meeting. Without the most basic shared norms such as respecting others' turns to speak and confidentiality, it is almost impossible to engender an atmosphere in which people are comfortable sharing their most personal feelings. Other rules, such as whether smoking is permitted in the meeting room, can be set later by members. By leaving the somewhat less essential ground rules open for discussion at the first meeting, participants feel more empowered.

Influenced strongly by the efforts of other self-help support groups, Mrs. Lindsey and Ms. Nichols defined the group's main objective or mission and set forth a few basic ground rules. The former was fairly easy, as they both had a common vision of the group's purpose, a purpose that they had shared with potential members who called for information. The mission of the "Morningside Women's Group," as they had dubbed themselves, was to provide aging and older women, regardless of race or religion, with a forum for sharing their hardships and joys in a mutually supportive, confidential, and democratic environment and to create opportunities for personal and group empowerment and growth. In the spirit of group empowerment, Mrs. Lindsey and Ms. Nichols did not want members to be confronted with a laundry list of rules and regulations; however, a few were deemed necessary to prevent potential problems. Ground rules to be presented at the first meeting included the following:

- *Complete and total confidentiality (nothing discussed within the confines of the group meetings was to be shared with nonmembers)*
- *Respect for others' comments (when one member is speaking, the others should be attentive and not interrupt)*
- *Equal opportunity (members and the facilitator have a responsibility to control monopolizers and encourage the more quiet members to contribute)*
- *Respect for members' diverse points of view (the goal of the group is not to reach consensus on matters, but rather to benefit from a broad array of viewpoints)*

- *Empowerment and democracy (to advance the goal of individual and group empowerment, all facets of the organization's operations are open to discussion and revision
  based on consensus of majority rule)*

*The two women were hopeful that the group, once established, would be instrumental in
creating a list of discussion topics. To get things started, however, an agenda for the first
5 weeks, open to revision, was developed.*

WEEK 1   *Introductions: To begin developing group cohesion, members were randomly
            paired, given an opportunity to get to know each other, and asked to intro-
            duce their partners rather than themselves.*
            Orientation to meeting facilities
            Group purpose
            Why a group for older women?
            Ground rules
            Review of meeting schedule and group duration
            Future discussion topics
            Each member's anticipated benefits of participation
WEEK 2   *The best things about being an aging–older woman*
            Challenges faced by aging–older women
            What makes aging–older women a unique group?
WEEK 3   *Favorite childhood memories*
            Most interesting moments in history
            How is life different today than years ago?
WEEK 4   *Health concerns of aging–older women*
            The formal medical establishment
            Informal supports in times of infirmity
WEEK 5   *Who is our "family" (biological and chosen)?*
            The role we play in our families (what we offer)
            What our families offer us
            In what ways could family relationships be improved
            (Ask for small donations to cover expenses)

At this phase in the planning process, one does not know whether the group
will be relatively passive and look to the leadership for session topics or if they will
want to be more actively involved in structuring their program. Thus, it is necessary
to have session plans in place for several weeks with the understanding that any or
all may be tossed aside in favor of alternatives proposed by the group.

Gathering information on group participants in advance can prove quite helpful
at this point. Without a knowledge of members' marital status, it is not clear whether
a discussion of widowhood would be appropriate. Similarly, a session dedicated
to retirement would likely lose the interest of lifelong homemakers or long-time retirees. Even given a familiarity with membership, session topics should be titled
and described in broad terms designed to be inviting to a broad array of women.
Thus, rather than offering a session on widowhood, a meeting could focus on
family relationships. On the basis of the outcome of such a meeting, a subsequent
discussion might highlight widowhood, marital relationships, or living alone, as
appropriate.

The week preceding the first meeting, details were ironed out. Ms. Nichols confirmed room availability for the designated days and times and checked the room for an adequate number of adult-size chairs and a table for refreshments. Mrs. Lindsey asked the church office manager if they would be willing to provide juice and cookies as the group had no operating budget at this time, a request that was readily granted. A comfortable sitting area was chosen for the aide who would accompany one member, but not stay for the group session. Group members were called to remind them of the first meeting and to reconfirm directions to the church. The morning of the first meeting, two signs were hung in the facility directing participants to the meeting room. The chairs in the classroom were arranged in a circle to facilitate interaction.

Finally, the day of the first meeting arrived. Ms. Nichols gave each participant a name tag and a warm welcome as she entered the room. She and Mrs. Lindsey tried to make small talk with the others as they waited for the remainder to arrive, but most were awkwardly quiet. The founding women retained their composure and exuded an air of confidence and calm, helping to keep the atmosphere in the room comfortable despite the lack of banter. As soon as the last to arrive settled in, Mrs. Lindsey warmly and enthusiastically welcomed the women and introduced herself. The introduction process that allowed each member to get to know and introduce her "partner," another member, broke the ice successfully. Each woman was asked to present the following information, at least, about her new acquaintance: name, hometown or place of birth, favorite hobbies or activities, reason for joining the Morningside Women's Group, and "What always makes me laugh is . . . ."

Ms. Nichols wrote the above list on the blackboard, which allowed Mrs. Lindsey to continue in her role as facilitator without interruption. The latter also walked casually around the room as the pairs were becoming acquainted to help the process along as needed. The exercise was an enormous success. Having each participant complete the sentence "What always makes me laugh is . . . ." was particularly useful in making people relax and share a smile. It additionally conveyed the important message that group meetings could be fun as well as purposeful. Although serious and even sad or unpleasant issues would be addressed, there would be ample opportunity for happiness and frivolity. With smiles on their faces following introductions, the women happily listened to Mrs. Lindsey's coverage of the remaining issues, and several even participated in the discussion.

Without exception, the first meeting of any self-help support group must be a success. Most of the membership typically will not make a final decision about continued participation until after the first gathering or even later. If a participant does not feel comfortable, welcome, or interested, she will most likely not return. There is no second chance. Naturally, it is important to make the first meeting as welcoming and universally appealing as possible, but there is an additional trick of the trade to making the group consider the session a success. As community organizers know, the leader should always end the first meeting with a few sentences about how successful the session has been. Those who have yet to form an opinion or who are unsure will often be convinced and return the following week.

Subsequent meetings proved to be equally successful, with only one woman not returning after the first session. The facilitator called her following her first absence to be sure she was well and, if she planned to leave the group, to ask why. In the event that something about the group was not satisfactory, the group could be changed accordingly or the member could be made to understand why this could not be done. In this particular case, however, the woman cited personal reasons unrelated to the support group. The group opted not to exercise the option of changing or rotating facilitators, and Mrs. Lindsey gladly retained the position.

Early on it became apparent that one member, Mrs. Ridge, consistently monopolized the conversation, annoying, offending, and inhibiting various other members. The facilitator recognized that her frequent comments were most often not the result of her need to ventilate and get feedback, but rather to gain attention. Fearing the other participants would lose interest as a result, Mrs. Lindsey politely and effectively managed the situation by responding to Mrs. Ridge's comments with an invitation to the rest of the group to address the issue raised. When this met with limited success, Mrs. Lindsey spoke with the monopolizing member after a session. She acknowledged the positive aspects of the input and engaged Mrs. Ridge's "assistance" in giving other members adequate opportunity to contribute to the discussions. By giving this member recognition and asking for her help, thereby treating her as a valued equal, Mrs. Lindsey was able to fulfill her need for acknowledgment and acclaim and reduce her need for such attention during meetings. Occasional follow-up conversations outside of group sessions augmented the initial intervention.

Handling both reluctant contributors and, at the other extreme, those who try to monopolize the discussions are two of the most common challenges faced by facilitators. The skilled group leader has the ability to pose questions and present leading statements that encourage everyone to contribute. If an individual does not speak up even after being invited to do so by the facilitator, the member can be approached privately after the meeting and asked in a nonthreatening manner what would help her feel more engaged or at ease during the meeting.

There are several ways to manage a monopolizer in the group. Those who are unaware of their behavior may become more sensitive to others' need to speak if the facilitator consistently curtails their comments and asks for others to comment on the point raised. In other situations it becomes necessary, as in the case of Mrs. Ridge, to speak to the offender privately. If these efforts meet with failure, groups have the option to add a ground rule about time limits on individuals' comments. This allows members to police each other, as all participants are empowered to enforce group norms.

Several weeks before a support group session addressing the issue of health concerns of aging and older women, the issue of bringing in a medical professional was raised. Those in favor of a guest speaker or facilitator cited the benefits of learning more about illnesses, symptoms, and state-of-the-art medications and treatments. The opposition noted their concerns about feeling comfortable talking about their feelings and fears related to illness and even death in front of an outsider, especially if the guest were to be a man. With two adamant camps, a compromise was ultimately reached that satisfied all parties. The topic would be handled in two separate sessions: one to share personal concerns in an environment of mutual support and another, led by a female medical practitioner, to learn more about older women's health matters and have specific questions answered.

The role of professionals in self-help support groups is hotly debated by both those in favor of their inclusion and those opposed who site the need for a purely indigenous organization. It is a matter best left to the discretion of each group, which can weigh the benefits of introducing an expert against the gains to be achieved from a strictly peer environment. Many organizations arrive at a middle ground where outsiders are afforded an occasional opportunity to facilitate or present information in a specialized area of interest.

One meeting of the Morningside Women's Group, dedicated to a discussion of long-term care options and preferences, unexpectedly erupted into a group conflict over members' differing financial capabilities and cultural norms related to family responsibility for caring for an incapacitated elder. One participant adamantly claimed "I'm never going to a nursing home . . . . I'd rather die at home . . . . I'll just get someone to come in and take care of me in my own home where I belong." This statement was quickly met with such responses (often in a sarcastic or angry tone) as "It must be nice to have that choice" and "Most of us don't have rich kids to pay for a caretaker like that!" Comments such as "I'm lucky to have a daughter who would never allow me to be sent off to a nursing home . . . . I'd live with her just like my mother lived with us" were countered with angry retorts such as "Well, I love my children and grandchildren too much to make them take care of me in one of their homes. I'm not such a selfish person . . . ." Others spoke of their ethnic heritage, which stressed the importance of filial responsibility. The association between ethnicity and values ignited a conflict fueled by defensiveness. All their fears related to chronic illness, deterioration, and long-term care boiled over in an attack on each other.

Mrs. Lindsey's escalating anxiety was not reflected in her calm demeanor. Her effort at regaining group cohesion began with a statement of the underlying emotional issues as she saw them. "Most of us are very frightened at the thought of needing someone else to take care of us . . . of being dependent on others for our basic daily needs and activities. I know I am. It's also scary because it is all so unpredictable. What condition will I be in? What kinds of things . . . even very personal care . . . will others have to do for me? Who will do these things? Will I be able to decide who cares for me or pay for needed care?" Mrs. Lindsey looked around the room for affirmation and, indeed, saw many nodding heads. To bring the group back together, she focused on commonalities. "Whether we are rich or poor . . . have family or not . . . come from different cultures . . . we all share an unknown future of health or illness, independence or dependence. I don't think we are really angry at each other, I think we are all scared. The other women in this room don't wish you illness and dependence, right?" Again, nods. "Yet you have the power to make the future better for yourselves and each other just by being there to listen, support, and care as you have been doing for months now." After giving the participants an opportunity to share thoughts and feelings about the positive roles they could fill for each other, Mrs. Lindsey steered the conversation to focus on the benefits of having different viewpoints and heritages in the group. Pointing out that there is no universal right or wrong long-term care solution, only an appropriate plan for each individual, she suggested that the group benefit from the richness of information and perspectives that differences allow. Eventually, calm was restored, and the women ended the session, at one member's urging, by holding hands as they sat in a circle and shared a moment of silent contemplation.

Before participants can be at ease with differences among them, especially those that concern deep-rooted beliefs and traditions, they must feel a group cohesion based on strong underlying commonalities. In a situation where conflict arises, it is critical to highlight the numerous characteristics, experiences, and feelings shared by the membership. Only then can those gathered begin to appreciate the value to be derived from the differences among them. For this reason, it is important to schedule the potentially inflammatory session plans for later in the group's life cycle, after a strong shared foundation has been laid.

After nearly 3 months of weekly sessions, the support group received startling and disturbing news. Ms. Dante, an easygoing member who was liked and respected by all, died suddenly and unexpectedly of a heart attack. Mrs. Lindsey received the news from the late member's niece and had the difficult task of informing the group. Rather than withholding the information until the end of the session, she deliberately presented the news at the beginning to give the group a chance to process the information, begin to mourn, and support each other while they were together.

After members freely shared their feelings about Ms. Dante and their sadness at her loss, the facilitator asked the group what, if anything, they would like to do as a group to acknowledge their peer's death. They agreed to postpone the day's topic, which would not allow them to vent their brimming feelings, and instead discuss death—both others' and their own—and concomitant feelings. Before departing for the day, all agreed to start the next session with a moment of silence in memory of their friend. Several made plans to attend the funeral together as well.

The death of a member is a twofold trauma for group members. It often represents the loss of a friend as well as a confrontation with one's own ultimate demise. Because this can be a highly emotional time for participants, it is important to offer the group an opportunity to acknowledge the loss and the concomitant feelings. Session plans should be placed on hold if members require a chance to mourn and cope together.

Over the first 12 weeks, the anticipated duration of the group, there was only minor change in the composition of the group. One woman was forced to resign owing to a relocation to Florida with her recently retired husband. Another woman, hearing about the group through word of mouth, joined the group in the fourth week on agreement by existing participants that a new member would be welcome. The group coalesced fairly quickly and easily despite slight changes in membership.

At the 10th session, with the projected final meeting in clear sight, the facilitator presented the group with its options: (a) continue with the current membership for a predetermined number of sessions, (b) continue with the current membership for an indefinite number of sessions, (c) recruit new members to rotate in to replace existing members who may choose to leave the group or to expand the size of the group and allow the new group to determine its duration, or (d) terminate altogether.

The women unanimously decided to continue with the current membership for another 12 weeks, the rationale being that it took several weeks for them to fully mesh as a group, and they wanted to reap the benefits of their bonds for an extended period of time.

The second 12-week period proved to be as successful as the first. The vast majority of the women had developed personal relationships with one or more other group members and frequently participated in social and recreational activities outside of the meeting times. Although not a source of conflict or discontent, a clear division emerged within the group. Three members had been widowed within the past 18 months and continued to have difficulty adjusting. They all used the group sessions as a forum for soliciting support. The other members were married, single, or widowed and not challenged by the same issues as the recent widows. One faction, therefore, wanted to focus on more upbeat issues without being "dragged down" to where some had been emotionally at another point in time. The other faction had a greater need to air the sources of unhappiness in their lives.

Thus, as the end of the second 12 weeks approached, there was no consensus as to the fate of the group. Without any hurt feelings or lack of agreement on the value of the group, five participants chose to leave the group and to continue to seek and give support to each other outside the parameters of a structured support group. As facilitator, Mrs. Lindsey dedicated the last session to termination. The group reviewed the mutual benefits reaped over the past several months and shared the newly acquired insights and strengths they would take away with them. The women also expressed their sadness about the end of the group, although its dissolution was planned.

Most self-help support groups end at some point or another, so it is critical that those involved recognize this as a natural transition—a growth—rather than as a failure. A meeting dedicated to termination should be scheduled to address the many benefits and gains achieved over the group's lifetime, both for individuals and for the group as a whole. Emphasis can be placed on relationships that evolved and now exist beyond the confines of the weekly sessions. Each individual's strengths with regard to coping with termination can be reviewed by the group. If the group's end is not the participants' choice but rather an imposed decision, it is essential to discuss other options for peer support, both formal and informal, available to members.

CONCLUSION

An overview of the life cycle of a self-help support group for women is a useful tool for group planners trying to conceptualize group composition and activities as well as to anticipate common hurdles. While there is no perfect template to apply to all groups, there are numerous commonalities across groups with which planners should be familiar. For this reason, it is useful, as previously noted, to acquire as much information as possible from established self-help support groups and organizations that assist or sponsor groups.

10

Recommendations for Promoting the Effectiveness of Self-Help Support Groups

In this summary chapter, conclusions are drawn from all phases of the research, and recommendations are offered for successfully planning, implementing, and maintaining self-help support group initiatives for older women. Attention is first directed toward the local analysis of the SOWN experience and is followed by consideration of the lessons to be learned from the national survey. Overall recommendations are offered, and final thoughts are then presented in the epilogue.

CONCLUSIONS AND RECOMMENDATIONS DRAWN FROM THE PHILADELPHIA ANALYSIS

SOWN's Efficacy

The assertions of Drake and D'Asaro presented in chapter 3 concerning the success of the SOWN model stand up exceedingly well under the scrutiny of systematic analysis. Although not without its expected challenges, the SOWN model has succeeded in no uncertain terms in drawing an expanding cohort of older women who have found their lives transformed for the better as a result of participation in self-help group activities. The continuous expansion of SOWN programming in the years before and after the period during which this research was initiated is testimony both to the legitimacy and popularity of the idea.

Profiling the Group Member

Although a significant proportion of SOWN women may already have participated in general group activities at the national, regional, or local levels, they are more likely to be newcomers to formal self-help programming, not commonly experiencing the benefits of mutual aid before joining a SOWN group. First learning about the SOWN program through the informal support network—that is, by means of personalized word of mouth—SOWN members are characterized most accurately as being White, in their mid-70s, retired, widowed, and in fair to good health. Interestingly, this is, in fact, also the classic profile of the older recipient of gerontological services in this country. However, it is notable that SOWN has been shown to appeal as well to a substantial number of African American older women, especially in urban settings.

Are there particular kinds of persons who are likely to benefit most from self-help group programs? In principle, most older women have the capacity to benefit from the process. However, those with persistent, if not overriding, mental and physical health problems might swallow up a group's energies. Participants need to have some degree of support and control over life's demands. Participants also need to be reasonably self-aware and not intent on imposing their own views on the group. Those who will benefit most seem to display some degree of comfort with group process and are willing to accept help from others. Individuals who are autonomous and independent to an extreme, are intolerant of others, and are very task oriented may experience frustrations in these groups. An appreciation of the rewards of group process is necessary, as is the capacity to identify with a group, share feelings and ideas, and communicate with others.

Profiling the Group Facilitator

Peer group facilitators are likely to be women in their 60s with stronger remaining ties to the workplace, surviving spouses, and additional measures of education and better health than other female members of the support groups. They do not generally have available the assistance of a cofacilitator, and, in their absence, other members of the group, when they are willing, fill in, assuming temporarily the functions of indigenous facilitators.

Are there particular qualities or skills that appear to be most important to those who organize or facilitate self-help support groups for older women? Our data suggest that the answer to this question is undoubtedly yes. Facilitators will realize greatest success if they have the capacity to remain objective and neutral in terms of what women "should" or "should not" be doing with their lives. A democratic perspective on leadership is desirable. A facilitator needs to recognize that women are going to display a variety of coping skills and, therefore, a diversity of coping responses to challenging situations. The skill of listening, that is, a genuine openness to hearing what is being said by others, is essential, as is the ability not to feel compelled to take action each time an issue surfaces. Recognition needs to be given to the problem-solving skills and capacities that the women themselves bring to the group. Group members need the opportunity to take action themselves. A Type A personality—one who is aggressive, domineering, controlling, and feels the need to get things done—is not likely to be one who will serve self-help group facilitators particularly well.

Facilitators will benefit from being patient, engaging, willing to deal with feelings, comfortable with sharing, warm, and caring and from having the motivation to help others. The possession of organizational and group work skills and problem-solving capacities are definite pluses. Obviously, a kinship with and affection for older people is desirable, as is respect for how much women have achieved in a sexist society. Facilitators will need to be able to accept vulnerability and, at times, helplessness in group members' lives. The women participating in self-help can be expected to have had to grapple with feelings of dependency and helplessness at various points in their lives and have probably not had a chance to acknowledge it in an open forum as much as they would have wished. The most successful facilitator will have the capacity to maximize the individuality of each group member at the same time that group cohesion and collectivity is fostered.

SOWN's Impact

For all women generally—and older, lower income, more educated African American women in particular—the SOWN concept has been received quite positively. SOWN programming would appear to have had a positive impact on members' overall well-being, personal self-esteem, integrity of social support networks, sense of connectedness to others, sense of being cared for, and happiness (Kaye, 1995b). Participating older women also have established frequent connections with SOWN members outside of the actual group meetings themselves. This is especially the case for African Americans. And members appear to want even more contact with their fellow participants between meetings. Perhaps this is indicative of an effort on their parts to continue to conceive of strategies by which to buttress the strength of their informal support networks during a period in their lives when loss has become a commonplace experience.

It is noteworthy that the educational level of the women in these support groups is relatively high, with the majority possessing a high school degree and a substantial minority holding either a bachelor's or a master's degree. In light of this level of educational achievement, the challenge for groups of this type may be, in addition to serving as a conduit for opportunities for social intimacy, to provide adequate intellectual stimulation to hold the commitment of members over the long term.

The experience of being a part of a SOWN group has been a positive, albeit demanding, one for peer facilitators as well. Facilitators have had to deal with disruptive, narcissistic and overly defensive participants. They have been challenged to stop members from damaging group process without turning them off to the experience. They have had to be supportive and search for desirable capacities in persons in order to bring them out and make them contributing members to group process.

It seems quite clear that the receipt of professional, yet personalized, assistance from SOWN staff has been a pivotal factor in making the experience a good one for these indigenous facilitators. Facilitators believe that more such aid on a personal, face-to-face basis from SOWN staff is not only desirable, but in fact essential if they are to carry out their group facilitation responsibilities with maximum effectiveness.

Furthermore, there is evidence to suggest that facilitators receive considerably less support and aid than is desirable from members of the groups themselves, especially in terms of the demanding task of identifying new topics or subject matter for the groups to address from one meeting to the next. It appears clear that stress reduction, reduced burnout, and increased effectiveness among the older women serving as peer facilitators will be best achieved by maintaining adequate levels of available technical assistance and training from SOWN staff, combined with inducing members to take more responsibility for ensuring the continuity of group process and function (e.g., engaging more readily in group cofacilitation and topic development functions).

Group dynamic issues proving to be particularly challenging for facilitators include balancing group member participation; dealing with disruptive, withdrawn, depressed, or distressed participants; maintaining group focus; and ensuring all participants share in the responsibilities of group operation. The more widespread sharing of group responsibilities is likely to be the best safeguard against entrenched vision and the burden of facilitation.

The value of group facilitation rather than group leadership has been emphasized throughout this analysis. The distinction is an important one given the characterization of these groups as being based on principles of self-help and empowerment. It is recognized, however, that some self-help support groups, based on the capacities of their membership, may require more prominent guidance by a designated individual or individuals. These same groups may require more active technical assistance from program professionals as well. Although as a rule minimal intervention and influence by professionals and facilitators is sought, there is the need for flexibility. At different points in time, professional assistance may need to be offered in the form of consultations, providing educational and informational materials, making special topic presentations, and even serving as group facilitators. Groups of women new to the experience of self-help who are having substantial difficulties focusing their efforts should not resist time-limited aid from those who are more skilled at group process.

The successful SOWN group is characterized by excitement and ongoing engagement of the issues. It meets regularly, often more than once a month, and values highly the benefits of group process. It is a living group that is genuine and authentic, allowing for different personalities and motivations to express themselves and relationships to develop. Risk taking is seen to be more important than acting conservatively. Participants are still growing in terms of who they are. They are experiencing continuous self-actualization, a process not fostered enough in a sexist society that underestimates the capacities of older women in terms of discovery and capacity to deal with issues. The self-help group that works is growth oriented. The common problems and issues confronted by members ultimately serve to unite these women. Empowerment for these women requires, apparently, a relational base. The development of relationships would appear to represent the glue of group process. During the course of their deliberations, power is shared among members and not wielded by a select few.

The Affective Rewards of SOWN Participation

The appeal and impact of SOWN has been primarily in the affective domain (apparently for both members and facilitators). That is, the attractiveness and potential of SOWN self-help support groups is greatest in terms of providing consistent opportunities for socialization, friendship and personal support network development, emotional support during times of crisis, and relationship building. Its appeal, and its efficacy in the instrumental domain (i.e., as an educational and informational forum) would appear to be considerably less pronounced.

In conclusion, data have confirmed that the SOWN experience (like self-help support group experiences generally) is less an intellectual encounter and more a profound emotional and social one. Although difficult and even painful at times for members who periodically come to share the feelings arising from the various losses associated with old age, SOWN's emphasis on emotional ventilation, and the fact that it embraces unfalteringly a support-inducing function, is pivotal in defining the benefits to be derived from this powerful mutual aid experience.

The Concept of Self-Help

Although the concept of self-help appears somewhat ambiguous in the minds of the support group members who were interviewed, about half of these individuals were convinced that the groups operate in this manner. Although most members were able to verbalize the value of SOWN meetings in various ways—from social and emotional support to an educational perspective, to a lesser degree—it is not clear that they comprehended the meaning of self-help as it was initially intended.

Much of the attractiveness of the SOWN concept appears to be that it incorporates so many different perspectives on aging as contributed by each individual member. In that process, self-help is activated and made operative within the group, and, on some level, the members are aware of its presence, even though they may be unable to conceptualize it completely.

During the course of our research, self-help, as enacted by SOWN groups, came to be reflected in group members' using their individual and collective strengths and competencies for problem solving and self-actualization.

The Emotional Challenge of Support Group Participation

The SOWN members talked to during the course of the project were obviously quite appreciative of the help and support they have received as a result of friendships established in SOWN. They seemed drawn together by the discussion of a range of topics, including family, children, the past, issues on aging, health, and current events. Just watching each of the members respond to the questions asked of them appears to have conveyed a renewed vitality to being part of a unique experience: a support group composed of older women.

Although it has been noted by many individuals spoken to during the course of the project that group members are reticent to discuss tragic events or feelings of loss, the evidence from comments regarding SOWN's effectiveness during major life changes indicates, in reality, a different experience. Many of the members stated that their major life changes—such as retirement, death of a family member, illness, financial strain, and nursing home placement of a member of the group—were easier to endure as a result of receiving SOWN members' advice and support.

The topic of loss is obviously a sensitive one for these women and appears to be defined as broadly encompassing all aspects of life change. For example, many members have had to downsize their living arrangements, and that process necessitated giving away many belongings. This was a common loss suffered by the members. Common, also, was the experience of widowhood, as well as the "thinning" of one's local social support network as a consequence of daughters and sons making the decision to move their immediate families to locations at a considerable distance from their parents' place of residence.

Agendas, Extragroup Interaction, and Group Process

Most facilitators indicated that their groups maintain an agenda, regardless of whether it is adhered to or whether their groups digress from it. The primary focus seems to be one directed at the feelings and problems of members, which can and do surface without any warning whatsoever. In this regard, many facilitators admitted to a sense of inadequacy in terms of their capacity to handle the group dynamics and requested additional training in this area. Support groups everywhere will want to consider the handling of such issues as pivotal to their long-term success.

Overall, there seemed to be agreement on the need for more interaction with the SOWN office staff, in terms of guidance with topics as well as specific problems. This is likely to represent a subtle, yet ongoing tension for self-help support group programmers and participants both in the SOWN network of groups and in older adult self-help support groups initiatives elsewhere. On the one hand, self-help support should be just that, support offered by and received from oneself and one's peers. On the other hand, for such groups to continue to function effectively, the assistance of professional group work personnel is likely to be necessary on a periodic basis. It may be most accurate to speak of these groups functioning best, in most cases, in semiautonomous fashion, in terms of the influence that will need to be wielded by self-help, gerontological, and group work professionals.

The importance of the interaction theme in the view of group members and facilitators is highlighted in other ways. There was the suggestion from several women that it would be highly desirable to intermingle with other SOWN groups throughout the city and in the process learn new topics as well as successful processes of conducting meetings and related activities. In similar fashion, it was observed by several women that two of the groups meet in the same building where there is a children's day care facility. Opportunities for intergenerational contact and exchange were described in very positive terms. Indeed, for these women, the opportunities for relationship building across generations appeared to have had an energizing effect on both individual members as well as the group as a whole.

Although several facilitators made it clear that they saw no need for change in terms of how their groups were operating, suggestions were offered by other facilitators, including starting the meeting on time more regularly; sharing more responsibility; maintaining more contact with the SOWN main office, including more visits from SOWN headquarters to the individual sites; and starting the group again, in centers where it had dwindled or disappeared altogether.

It is noteworthy that a majority of the group members talked to expressed not the need for any substantial changes, but additional testimony to the value of the group meetings. Those offering suggestions focused on revitalizing groups, either by re-starting groups that had floundered or recruiting new members to some of the smaller groups. There were a few suggestions on training, especially in terms of the value of understanding group dynamics more clearly. Another recommended more luncheon get-togethers. Finally, several group members and their facilitators noted that their respective groups needed to practice more respect for one another while sharing, giving others enough time to have their say, but at the same time putting limits on those who are determined to dominate the group process by talking too much.

CONCLUSIONS AND RECOMMENDATIONS DRAWN FROM THE NATIONAL SURVEY

In this section, the findings from the national survey of selected self-help group programs are summarized and synthesized into a description of the central elements of a model self-help program for older women.

The central purpose of self-help or peer support groups for older women is to create an opportunity for older adults to share experiences, thoughts, and problems with other older adults. Some programs believe that peer facilitation is an integral part of the self-help process. The model self-help group for older women empowers participants to make decisions for themselves and to help others with their problems. The Peer Support program of the Jackson County Department on Aging exemplifies this approach. According to the coordinator, the goal of the program is to assist senior citizens in making their own decisions. The peer facilitator training manual emphasizes that peer support volunteers are advised against giving advice. Chrysalis reiterated this theme, emphasizing mutual support in a feminist context. They express a commitment to helping each woman identify her own barriers to success, help her discover the strengths and resources required to take control of her life, and encourage her to accept the support of other women who made similar changes and decisions.

The majority of the groups studied at the national level serve only women. Data suggested that there is a great need for support groups serving older women, as women live longer than men and therefore more often experience loss and the psychological challenges related to loss. Mixed groups may also be beneficial for the men and women involved, especially when sensitive topics such as sexuality are discussed.

Groups involved in this study served women between the ages of 45 and 90 years of age. Findings emphasize that middle-aged women and older women face somewhat different sets of challenges and concerns. Programs should carefully consider the age parameters for their groups and think about creating separate groups for older and younger women.

The overwhelming number of older people participating in self-help groups are White, although some programs have realized significant inroads by the African American community. Outreach should be extended to Latino, Asian and Pacific Islander, Native American, and African American older women as well as other minority female groups. Reaching out successfully to these elderly women may well be a challenge, one in which a positive response is not immediately forthcoming given the strong tendency of this cohort to underuse health care services and programs (Hart, Gallagher-Thompson, Davies, DiMinno, & Lessin, 1996; Krause & Wray, 1991). Community needs assessments will likely have to be conducted to ensure that self-help group programming initiatives in these communities are responsive to the needs and concerns of the older residents residing there. Furthermore, self-help groups will need to remain mindful that their programming be sensitive to the language and nuances of the ethnic group in question in order to maximize cultural relevancy (Braun, Takamura, Forman, Sasaki, & Meininger, 1995; Gallagher-Thompson et al., 1994).

Successful groups market themselves at minimal cost through public service announcements and word of mouth. Another successful recruitment strategy is to educate doctors, clergy, and mental health professionals, who then refer older adults to groups. Whenever possible, groups should attempt to benefit from free media coverage and to use mixed media approaches while realizing that personal, face-to-face approaches to outreach are likely to be most effective. Groups should not depend on a single approach to communicate to the larger community who they are and what they do. Experience in the human services has shown that community and group presentations and in-person outreach are most effective in combination with the production of descriptive brochures and flyers.

Group self-help programs need to think seriously about the relative advantages and disadvantages of accepting financial support from funding sources that have established guidelines restricting fund recipients' freedom to seek support from other sources. On the one hand, self-help groups and their organizational representatives have operating costs that must be covered. On the other hand, groups may not want to depend on a single source of support for their livelihood.

Programs should include a screening process. This process will help to identify those people whose problems cannot be dealt with adequately in a group and will give program coordinators an opportunity to orient older adults to the group work concept.

Problems facing older people are vast and complex. For this reason, many programs offer ongoing groups. Data have suggested that ongoing groups are better able to meet the needs of older people than are time-limited groups. Groups numbering between 10 and 15 members are an ideal size for group sharing and interaction.

Peer facilitation offers benefits to both the facilitator and group member. Facilitators grow as they accept the responsibility of leading a support group. Facilitators also serve as role models for group members, who see that their peers are able to accept this important challenge successfully. The Senior Health and Peer Counseling Center has created a nationally recognized peer facilitation model that includes both individual peer counseling and group facilitation. Peer facilitation training programs are comprehensive and include didactic and experiential elements. Communication and facilitation skills, as well as substantive issues facing older adults, are explored. Peer facilitators should receive regular supervision from a trained professional and have opportunities to meet together to share experiences and problem solve.

Results of this analysis suggest that peer support groups are successful when the sessions are not excessively structured. However, facilitators have successfully introduced exercises that help members explore issues in greater depth and with greater thoughtfulness.

The topics addressed in peer support groups are numerous and varied. Topics include emotional issues such as how to cope with grief and confront one's mortality, practical issues such as how to manage money or maintain one's home, and social issues such as sexuality and companionship. Group members benefit from discussing a broad range of issues that encompass the various aspects of aging in our society.

None of the groups studied emphasized the creation of informal support networks. In some, members are encouraged to call one another, whereas in others, this is actually discouraged. If self-help programs aim to minimize the isolation of older adults, they may want to more explicitly encourage group members to build relationships outside of sessions, as does SOWN.

Overall Program Recommendations

Several overall program-specific recommendations have been formulated on the basis of the responses received and observations made during the research. They apply to all such programs like SOWN that are seeking to maximize the efficacy of the self-help support group concept for older women.

First, ensure that adequate guidance is offered to group members and facilitators in the following areas in particular:

- understanding group dynamics, interpersonal skills, and group leadership approaches
- undergoing practical training, especially for volunteer facilitators, in areas such as developing group topics and setting agendas
- where appropriate, organizing regional or centralized meetings for facilitators on a regularly scheduled basis
- planning activities to promote interaction and increased sharing of responsibility among similar such groups and their members
- ensuring extensive monitoring of the efforts of new group facilitators, until they feel comfortable in their positions
- providing group members with community service materials and directories that enable them to make their own formal service utilization decisions. Such directories can increase service awareness and prompt independent decisions by elders regarding use (Cherry, Prebis, & Pick, 1995).

Second, although professional assistance in the above areas is desirable, program personnel need to remain mindful of the principles of self-help and respect the group and its members' need to struggle through the process of survival to a significant degree on their own.

Third, the use of volunteers in group self-help is to be encouraged. Given limitations in likely sources of external financial support, individuals with voluntaristic spirits can be most helpful. Hopefully, such individuals will be drawn from populations that are indigenous to the cohort being served by a particular self-help support group. Programmers do need to be mindful that the use of volunteers does have its inevitable costs and obligations in terms of the training, supervision, monitoring, and recognition such individuals will require.

Fourth, organizations engaged in group self-help may find the placement of students in the allied health and human service professions a source of important support. Professional social work, nursing, gerontology, and human service programs will likely find self-help group project initiatives to represent legitimate sites for student training. Once again, however, an organization must be ready to commit adequate resources in the form of supervisory field instruction for such an arrangement to succeed.

The Skills and Methods of Group Work

Both professional staff and peer group facilitators have available to them considerable resources that address the foundation knowledge required to organize, operate, and maintain self-help support groups for older women. A variety of how-to manuals and training programs are listed in appendix B. In addition, a series of recently published group methods and skills texts are available that address either group process generally or older adult group process in particular. They deal with such issues as group dynamics, leadership strategies, and phases of elder group development (Toseland, 1995; Bertcher, 1993), dealing with diversity in groups

(Feit, Ramey, Wodarski, & Mann, 1995), membership recruitment techniques and conducting first group meetings (Bertcher & Maple, 1996), operating groups in a troubled society (Kurland & Salmon, 1995), dealing with elder isolation and reduced social network in group contexts (Erwin, 1996), and support group practice principles (Galinsky & Schopler, 1996). Although these texts do not necessarily focus precisely on self-help group process or the experiences of older women in such groups, the principles of group work that are addressed nevertheless have considerable application value. Group facilitators and program staff may also want to keep abreast of group practice materials published in such professional journals as *Social Work with Groups, Journal of Gerontological Social Work, International Journal of Group Psychotherapy,* and *Groupwork.*

Reminiscence and Life Review

Although not conceived of as a form of group therapy per se, group self-help may be said to represent a therapeutic event for many of its participants: a form of self- or peer-performed therapy. Peer facilitators and group members may find a modified version of the technique of reminiscence or life review to be a therapeutic strategy worth using in more systematic fashion in their groups. This process is increasingly believed to reflect a natural event in a person's life having considerable therapeutic benefit. Reminiscence therapy entails a systematic review of one's life, resulting in a coming to terms with one's past life in order to prepare for the remaining years of life. Such a review of life experience encourages an individual to reduce any conflict that may exist between present and past experiences of self. The process, when successful, results in a reaffirmation of identity and self-esteem and an increase in feelings of self-worth and ego integrity, enabling the older person to reengage in life. Given its adaptive function, reminiscence can lead to the reestablishment of social relationships and the integration of a person's total life experience. Put differently, a potential benefit of reminiscence is a decrease in the dissonance between past and present self (Fielden, 1990, 1992; Tarnowski, 1996).

Of course, as an evocative process, facilitators should be prepared for reminiscence to evoke depressive as well as positive affect on the part of group participants. Reminiscence is usually, but not always, an enjoyable process. For elderly people, just having memories implies a loss of what has been experienced at an earlier point in one's life. These feelings of loss may, on occasion, lower mood. Expressions of sadness and even depression, however, need not be avoided, even in a self-help support group. There may well be benefit, in fact, to having members fully experience the sadness associated with reminiscence rather than having them try to avoid it. In this context, coping constructively with feelings of sadness is conceived of as a desirable and necessary developmental accomplishment in an older person's life. Ultimately, increased life satisfaction and enhanced self-esteem can be the consequence of remembering and then working through negative as well as positive feelings associated with past experiences.

Reminiscence in groups requires a relatively active and exceedingly enthusiastic group facilitator or leader. It is hoped that people's enthusiasm will be contagious. In addition, facilitators should be respectful of what group members know and have experienced. Group members should be informed that the information they have been willing to reveal is instructive. Recognizing the educative value of personal disclosures enables members to assume the role of teacher, which can be self-esteem building in itself. Certainly it is essential that members of the group understand that their lives and experiences are valuable and that what they remember can be instructive to others (Tarnowski, 1996).

In conducting a reminiscence or life review session, it is recommended that themes not be too broad in nature. Participants may respond more readily to a narrow or circumscribed topic that requires less prompting and enables more group participation. It is also suggested that emphasis be on topics that focus directly on group members' personal memories rather than on a particular period of time. Finally, facilitators will want to encourage group members to be imaginative when reminiscing. For example, members can be asked to close their eyes; picture a person, place, or event; and then describe what they "see." This procedure can result in memories becoming much more vivid and alive (Tarnowski, 1996). For group members experiencing some degree of cognitive impairment and, therefore, difficulties in processing information, visual aids and other forms of creative sensory stimulation (i.e., feeling, tasting, touching, hearing, and seeing exercises) may prove helpful (Ott, 1993).

Burnside (1995) advocated the use of props and themes as tools to elicit memories from group members as well as a time line spanning the older person's life. She warned that such materials may be especially effective with persons suffering from cognitive deficits; however, she also noted that the use of too many props and similar devices may produce sensory overload for group members, especially those experiencing varying degrees of memory loss. Other tools and techniques worth considering when conducting reminiscence groups with older adults include the use of guided autobiographies (de Vries, Birren, & Deutchman, 1995), special methods of telling one's story (Thorsheim & Roberts, 1995), the Life Challenges Interview (Rybarczyk, 1995), and the Life Review and Experiencing Form (Haight, Coleman, & Lord, 1995). Haight and Webster (1995) offer one of the most current and definitive resources for those working in the field of reminiscing.

EPILOGUE

There is considerable evidence to suggest that an active and rapidly expanding self-help movement is afoot in this country. Millions of Americans consider themselves to be members of self-help groups on any given day in the United States. If interested, there is likely to be a self-help group in one's community that will be of assistance in confronting the difficulties associated with a vast array of personal and family problems and crises, including obesity, vision impairment, alcohol and narcotics addictions, mental illness, heart disease, cancer, depression, widowhood, and caring for a frail relative. For example, a national survey of self-help and mutual aid support groups for visually impaired older people identified 406 such groups alone in 48 states, the District of Columbia, and Puerto Rico (Lighthouse National Center for Vision and Aging, 1992). Self-help clearinghouses, which provide self-help program information and referral assistance for both the general public and the professional community, have been established in all regions of the country and in most major cities. Even the University of Michigan has established a Center for Self-Help

Research and Knowledge Dissemination, which carries out formal research with the goal of better understanding the relationship between self-help efforts and the professional service community.

Despite the apparent popularity of the current self-help movement, the distinctive character and process of mutual aid groups are still far from being fully understood. Various authors have pointed to significant variation in terms of the structure, nature of relationship with professionals and formal systems, and kinds of help provided by such groups (Borkman, 1990; Powell, 1994; Riessman & Carroll, 1995). There appear to be at least four broad types of mutual aid: that dealing with compulsive behaviors and emotional problems (Kurtz, 1990b), that dealing with family support needs (Medvene, 1990), that dealing with issues of health and disability (Katz & Maida, 1990), and that dealing with matters of death, dying, and bereavement (e.g., widowhood, death of a child; Videka-Sherman, 1990). Other categories of self-help can be expected to emerge in the years ahead.

Self-help groups, although different in many respects, do display a strong tendency to be single-issue oriented. That is, they focus their attention on an extremely focused and finite set of related issues (such as widowhood or elder caregiving). Groups that are determined to deal with the broad set of concerns facing a particular cohort of Americans (such as those studied in this research) remain the exception to the rule. The idea of generic self-help support groups for older women, charged with dealing with the myriad of problems and challenges associated with female aging, has not yet been widely adopted. Yet, findings presented here strongly suggest that multipurpose mutual aid for a special subgroup of older adults (in this case, older women) has been well received by those choosing to participate and can be quite efficacious.

Older women's self-help programming, although still variously characterized, designed, and implemented, is a legitimate and much desirable element of the gerontological services network that is, as yet, grossly underdeveloped. Furthermore, the SOWN concept (focused on especially in this analysis), and others like it in other regions of the country, are worthy of being considered seriously for replication in communities throughout the United States. Examples of similar such mutual aid programming initiatives are only now beginning to surface in communities outside of the Philadelphia metropolitan area. Unfortunately, funds supporting the development of self-help programming for older women remain extremely scarce. Monies in support of self-help programming that would direct attention to issues of legislative advocacy and clinical interventions are likely to be even more difficult to come by. As a result, it is anticipated that consumer need will continue to outstretch organizational and institutional capacity in this area.

As has been underscored throughout this book, the consequences of the aging process and of old age present particular challenges for women. The ability to address those challenges can only be enhanced if more women have available to them an adequate range of intervention strategies, including those that lie outside the traditional domain of the formal and largely professionalized social welfare system. Those strategies that are not wholly dependent on the services of professionals can represent a critical set of supplemental supports for older women.

Group self-help may be particularly attractive given the chronic scarcity of social service program dollars. Self-help as a resource-conserving strategy cannot be overlooked. In this period of resource scarcity, any intervention that conserves the use of public dollars has to be looked at seriously. At the same time as self-help initiatives appear to be efficient programming entities from a financial standpoint, they also stand to offer women the special opportunity to realize a significant bolstering of their self-esteem, competence, and morale in the absence of continuous, and seemingly unnecessary, professional influence.

Perhaps the overriding appeal of the self-help paradigm and mutual aid programming strategies is the opportunity for participating women to marshal their own resources and capacities without inordinate professional inducement. A strong argument can be mounted concerning the impact of the interface of ageism and sexism on older women. Older women remain unquestionably a population that is, at a minimum, at risk and not infrequently oppressed (Browne, 1995).

Carolyn Heilbrun, a feminist scholar and author of a major biography of Gloria Steinem as well as the book *Reinventing Womanhood,* advocate for mid-life women (those 50 years and over) to question everything and seek to achieve greater autonomy (Mulligan, 1996). Heilbrun spoke of a needed transformation in women's lives. She believed that entry into the middle years represents an excellent opportunity for women to achieve a renewed sense of inner worth and purpose. However, such a transformation is not going to be realized if women do not assume responsibility for their own lives and accept, at the same time, certain amounts of danger and risk (Mulligan, 1996). Perhaps this reason alone, the opportunity for a woman's personal transformation and empowerment, is adequate justification to sound an enthusiastic appeal to expand mutual aid programming for older women and other special cohorts of at-risk older Americans.

References

AARP Women's Initiative. (1994a). *Facts about older women: Housing and living arrangements* (fact sheet). Washington, DC: American Association of Retired Persons.

AARP Women's Initiative. (1994b). *Facts about older women: Income and poverty* (fact sheet). Washington, DC: American Association of Retired Persons.

AARP Women's Initiative. (1994c). *Midlife and older divorced women: A financial snapshot* (fact sheet). Washington, DC: American Association of Retired Persons.

AARP Women's Initiative. (1994d). *Twelve powerful facts about older women* (fact sheet). Washington, DC: American Association of Retired Persons.

AARP Women's Initiative. (1994e). *Women's health issues: Taking action* (fact sheet). Washington, DC: American Association of Retired Persons.

AARP Women's Initiative. (1996a). *The contingent workforce: Implications for today's and tomorrow's midlife and older women* (fact sheet). Washington, DC: American Association of Retired Persons.

AARP Women's Initiative. (1996b). *This could save your life: What all midlife and older women need to know about HIV/AIDS* (fact sheet). Washington, DC: American Association of Retired Persons.

Abramovitz, M. (1988). *Regulating the lives of women.* Boston: South End Press.

Achenbaum, W. A. (1986). *Social security: Visions and revisions.* Cambridge, MA: Cambridge University Press.

Adams, R. G. (1985). Emotional closeness and physical distance between friends: Implications for elderly women living in age-segregated and age-integrated settings. *International Journal of Aging and Human Development, 22,* 55–76.

Adams, R. G. (1987). Patterns of network change: A longitudinal study of friendships of elderly women. *The Gerontologist, 27,* 222–227.

American Cancer Society. (1992). *Cancer facts and figures.* Atlanta, GA: American Cancer Society.

Angel, J. L., & Hogan, D. P. (1991). The demography of minority aging populations. In Gerontological Society of America (Ed.), *Minority elders: Longevity, economics, and health—Building a public policy base* (pp. 1–13). Washington, DC: Gerontological Society of America.

Antze, P. (1976). The role of ideologies in peer psychotherapy organizations: Some theoretical considerations and three case studies. *Journal of Applied Behavioral Science, 12,* 323–346.

Atchley, R. C. (1997). *Social forces and aging: An introduction to social gerontology* (8th ed.). Belmont, CA: Wadsworth.

Babchuck, N. (1978). Aging and primary relationships. *International Journal of Aging and Human Development, 9,* 137–151.

Barnum, P., Liden, R. C., & DiTomaso, N. (1995). Double jeopardy for women and minorities. *Academy of Management Journal, 38,* 863–880.

Bear, M. (1990). Social networks and health: Impact on returning home after entry into residential care homes. *The Gerontologist, 30,* 30–34.

Bengston, V. L., Rosenthal, C., & Burton, L. (1990). Families and aging: Diversity and heterogeneity. In R. H. Binstock & L. K. George (Eds.), *Handbook of aging and the social sciences* (3rd ed., pp. 263–287). New York: Academic Press.

Benokraitis, N. (1987). Older women and reentry problems: The case of displaced homemakers. *Journal of Gerontological Social Work, 10,* 75–92.

Berkowitz, M. W., Waxman, R., & Yaffe, L. (1988). The effects of a resident self-help model on control, social involvement and self-esteem among the elderly. *The Gerontologist, 28,* 620–624.

Bertcher, H. J. (1993). *Group participation: Techniques for leaders and members* (2nd ed.). Thousand Oaks, CA: Sage Publications.

Bertcher, H. J., & Maple, F. F. (1996). *Creating groups* (2nd ed.). Thousand Oaks, CA: Sage Publications.

Blieszner, R. (1989). Developmental processes of friendship. In R. G. Adams & R. Blieszner (Eds.), *Older adult friendship.* Newbury Park, CA: Sage.

Borkman, T. J. (1990). Experiential, professional, and lay frames of reference. In T. J. Powell (Ed.), *Working with self-help* (pp. 3–30). Silver Spring, MD: NASW Press.

Bould, S., Sanborn, B., & Reif, L. (1989). *Eighty-five plus: The oldest old.* Belmont, CA: Wadsworth.

Braun, K., Takamura, J., Forman, S., Sasaki, P., & Meininger, L. (1995). Developing and testing outreach materials on Alzheimer's disease for Asian and Pacific Islander Americans. *The Gerontologist, 35,* 122–126.

Brody, E. M., Hoffman, C., Kleban, M. H., & Schoonover, C. B. (1989). Caregiving daughters and their local siblings: Perceptions, strains, and interactions. *The Gerontologist, 29,* 529–538.

Brody, J. (1992, February 15). Maintaining friendships for the sake of your health. *The New York Times,* p. 14.

Browne, C. V. (1995). Empowerment in social work practice with older women. *Social Work, 40,* 358–364.

Buhler, P. M. (1992). Managing in the 90s. *Supervision, 53,* 22–24.

Burnside, I. (1995). Themes and props: Adjuncts for reminiscence therapy groups. In B. K. Haight & J. D. Webster (Eds.), *The art and science of reminiscing: Theory, research, methods, and applications* (pp. 153–163). Washington, DC: Taylor & Francis.

Cain, B. S. (1988). Divorce among elderly women: A growing social phenomenon. *Social Casework, 69,* 563–568.

Cameron, K., Jorgenson, J., & Kawecki, C. (1993). Civil service 2000 revisited: Old assumptions—New facts and forecasts. *Public Personnel Management, 22,* 669–674.

Carroll, D. (1994). Self-help and the new health agenda. *Social Policy, 24*, 44–52.

Cath, S. (1971). Some dynamics of middle and later years. In H. Parad (Ed.), *Crisis intervention*. New York: Family Service Society.

Cherry, R. L., Prebis, J., & Pick, V. (1995). Service directories: Reinvigorating a community resource for self-care. *The Gerontologist, 35*, 560–563.

Choi, N. G., & Wodarski, J. S. (1996). The relationship between social support and health status of elderly people: Does social support slow down physical and functional deterioration? *Social Work Research, 20*, 52–63.

Cicirelli, V. G. (1985). The role of siblings as family caregivers. In W. J. Sauer & R. T. Coward (Eds.), *Social support networks and the care of the elderly* (pp. 93–107). New York: Springer.

Commonwealth Fund Commission. (1987). *Old, alone, and poor: A plan for reducing poverty among elderly people living alone*. Baltimore: The Commonwealth Fund Commission on Elderly People Living Alone.

Commonwealth Fund Commission. (1988). *Aging alone: Profiles and projections*. Baltimore: The Commonwealth Fund Commission on Elderly People Living Alone.

Conway, K. (1985). Coping with the stress of medical problems among black and white elderly. *International Journal of Aging and Human Development, 21*, 39–48.

Coward, R. T., Horne, C., & Dwyer, J. W. (1992). Demographic perspectives on gender and family caregiving. In J. W. Dwyer & R. T. Coward (Eds.), *Gender, families, and elder care*. Newbury Park, CA: Sage.

Davis, K., & Rowland, D. (1990). Old and poor: Policy challenges in the 1990s. *Journal of Aging and Social Policy, 2*, 37–59.

de Vries, B., Birren, J. E., & Deutchman, D. E. (1995). Method and uses of the guided autobiography. In B. K. Haight. & J. D. Webster (Eds.), *The art and science of reminiscing: Theory, research, methods, and applications* (pp. 165–177). Washington, DC: Taylor & Francis.

Drake, M., & Supportive Older Women's Network. (1993). *The power of support: A guide for creating self-help support groups for older women* (2nd ed.). Philadelphia: Supportive Older Women's Network.

Employee Benefit Research Institute. (1994). *Characteristics of the part-time work force: Analysis of the March 1993 current population survey* (Special Report and Issue Brief No. 149, SR-22, May 1994). Washington, D.C.: Employee Benefit Research Institute.

Erwin, K. T. (1996). *Group techniques for aging adults: Putting geriatric skills enhancement into practice*. Washington, DC: Taylor & Francis.

Feit, M. D., Ramey, J. H., Wodarski, J. S., & Mann, A. R. (1995). *Capturing the power of diversity*. Binghamton, NY: Haworth Press.

Fielden, M. A. (1990). Reminiscence as a therapeutic intervention with sheltered housing residents: A comparative study. *British Journal of Social Work, 20*, 21–44.

Fielden, M. A. (1992). Depression in older adults: Psychological and psychosocial approaches. *British Journal of Social Work, 22*, 291–307.

Friedman, E. (1993). Old and in the way. *Healthcare Forum, 36*, 10–13.

Galen, M. (1993, June 28). Work and family. *Business Week*, pp. 80–88.

Galinsky, M. J., & Schopler, J. H. (1996). *Support groups: Current perspectives on theory and practice*. Binghamton, NY: Haworth Press.

Gallagher-Thompson, D., Moorehead, R., Polich, T., Arguello, D., Johnson, C., Rodriguez, V., & Meyer, M. (1994). Comparison of outreach strategies for Hispanic caregivers of Alzheimer's victims. *Clinical Gerontologist, 15*, 57–63.

Garvin, C. (1984). The changing contexts of social group work practice: Challenge and opportunity. *Social Work with Groups, 7*, 3–19.

Gonyea, J. G. (1994). The paradox of the advantaged elder and the feminization of poverty. *Social Work, 39*, 35–41.

Gottlieb, B. H. (Ed.). (1981). *Social networks and social support*. Beverly Hills, CA: Sage.

Grad, S. (1992). *Income of the population 55 or older* (SSA Publication No. 13-11871, April 1992). Washington, DC: Social Security Administration, Office of Research and Statistics.

Grau, L. (1987). Illness-engendered poverty among the elderly. *Women and Health, 12*, 103–118.

Greene, E. (1992, April 21). For elderly women, a chance to talk. *The Chronicle of Philanthropy, 6*, 10.

Gutierrez, L., Ortega, R. M., & Suarez, Z. E. (1990). Self-help and the Latino community. In J. T. Powell (Ed.), *Working with self-help* (pp. 218–236). Silver Spring, MD: NASW Press.

Haight, B. K., Coleman, P., & Lord, K. (1995). The linchpins of a successful life review: Structure, evaluation, and individuality. In B. K. Haight. & J. D. Webster (Eds.), *The art and science of reminiscing: Theory, research, methods, and applications* (pp. 179–192). Washington, DC: Taylor & Francis.

Haight, B. K., & Webster, J. D. (Eds.). (1995). *The art and science of reminiscing: Theory, research, methods, and applications*. Washington, DC: Taylor & Francis.

Hart, V. R., Gallagher-Thompson, D., Davies, H. D., DiMinno, M., & Lessin, P. J. (1996). Strategies for increasing participation of ethnic minorities in Alzheimer's disease diagnostic centers: A multifaceted approach in California. *The Gerontologist, 36*, 259–262.

Hatch, L. R. (1991). Informal support patterns of older African-American and White women: Examining effects of family, paid work, and religious participation. *Research on Aging, 13*, 144–170.

Haug, M. R., & Folmar, S. J. (1986). Longevity, gender, and life quality. *Journal of Health and Social Behavior, 27*, 332–345.

Himes, C. L. (1992). Social demography of contemporary families and aging. *Generations, 16*, 13–16.

Hooyman, N. R. (1997). Is aging more problematic for women than men? Yes. In A. E. Scharlach & L. W. Kaye (Eds.), *Current controversies in aging* (pp. 126–130). Needham Heights, MA: Allyn & Bacon.

Hooyman, N. R., & Kiyak, H. A. (1988). *Social gerontology: A multidisciplinary perspective*. Needham Heights, MA: Allyn & Bacon.

Jacobs, R. H. (1990). Friendships among older women. *Journal of Women and Aging, 2*, 19–32.

Jendrek, M. P. (1992, September). *Grandparents who provide care to grandchildren: Preliminary findings and policy issues*. Paper presented at the annual meeting of Sociologists for Women in Society, Pittsburgh, PA.

Jorgensen, L. A. B. (1993). Public policy, health care and older women. *Journal of Women and Aging, 5,* 3–4.

Kart, C. S., & Dunkle, R. E. (1989). Assessing capacity for self-care among the aged. *Journal of Aging and Health, 1,* 430–450.

Kart, C. S., & Engler, C. A. (1994). Predisposition to self-health care: Who does what for themselves and why? *Journal of Gerontology: Social Sciences, 49,* S301–S308.

Kart, C. S., & Engler, C. A. (1995). Self-health care among the elderly: A test of the health-behavior model. *Research on Aging, 17,* 434–458.

Katz, A. H., & Bender, E. I. (Eds.). (1976). *The strength in us: Self-help in the modern world.* New York: Franklin Watts.

Katz, A. H., & Maida, C.A. (1990). Health and disability self-help organizations. In T. J. Powell (Ed.), *Working with self-help.* Silver Spring, MD: NASW Press.

Kaye, L. W. (1994). The effectiveness of services marketing: Perceptions of executive directors of gerontological programs. *Administration in Social Work, 18,* 69–85.

Kaye, L. W. (1995a). An analysis of promotional materials used by health and social service programs for older adults. *Journal of Nonprofit & Public Sector Marketing, 3,* 17–31.

Kaye, L. W. (1995b). Assessing the efficacy of a self-help support group program for older women. *Journal of Women and Aging, 7,* 11–30.

Kaye, L. W. (1996a). *Development of an economic model for a telemedicine system in home health care.* Report prepared for Tevital Inc., Paoli, PA.

Kaye, L. W. (1996b). Patterns of targeting and encouraging participation of elder consumers in human services marketing. *Health Marketing Quarterly, 13,* 27–46.

Kaye, L. W., & Applegate, J. S. (1990a). *Men as caregivers to the elderly.* Lexington, MA: Lexington Books.

Kaye, L. W., & Applegate, J. S. (1990b). Men as elder caregivers: A response to changing families. *American Journal of Orthopsychiatry, 60,* 86–95.

Kincade Norburn, J. E., Bernard, S. L., Konrad, T. R., Woomert, A., DeFriese, G. H., Kalsbeek, W. D., Koch, G. G., & Ory, M. G. (1995). Self-care and assistance from others in coping with functional status limitations among a national sample of older adults. *Journal of Gerontology: Social Sciences, 50B,* S101–S109.

Kirkland, R. I. (1994). Why we will live longer ... and what it will mean. *Fortune, 129,* 66–77.

Kleyman, P. (September–October 1995). Budget cutters set "policy agenda" for older women. *Aging Today,* p. 5.

Kostyk, D., Fuchs, D., Tabisz, E., & Jacyk, W. R. (1993). Combining professional and self-help group intervention: Collaboration in co-leadership. *Social Work with Groups, 16,* 111–23.

Kouri, M. K. (1984). From retirement to re-engagement: Young elders forge new futures. *Futurist, 18,* 35–42.

Krause, N., & Borawski-Clark, E. (1994). Clarifying the functions of social support in later life. *Research on Aging, 16,* 251–279.

Krause, N., & Wray, L. (1991). Psychosocial correlates of health and illness among minority elders. *Generations, 15,* 25–30.

Kurland, R., & Salmon, R. (1995). *Group work practice in a troubled society: Problems and opportunities.* Binghamton, NY: Haworth Press.

Kurtz, L. F. (1990a). The self-help movement: Review of the past decade of research. *Social Work With Groups, 13*, 101–111.

Kurtz, L. F. (1990b). Twelve step programs. In J. T. Powell (Ed.), *Working with self-help* (pp. 93–119). Silver Spring, MD: NASW Press.

Lang, N. (1981) Some defining characteristics of the social work group: Unique social form. In S. L. Abels. & P. Abels (Eds.), *Social work with groups* (Proceedings of 1979 symposium; pp. 18–50). Louisville, KY: Committee for the Advancement of Social Work with Groups.

Lee, G. R., & Shehan, C. L. (1989). Social relations and the self-esteem of older persons. *Research on Aging, 11*, 427–442.

Levine, M. (1988). How self-help works. *Social Policy, Summer, 19*, 39–43.

Levine, M., & Perkins, D. (1987). *Principles of community psychology*. New York: Oxford University Press.

Levy, L. (1976). Self-help groups: Types and psychological processes. *Journal of Applied Behavioral Science, 12*, 310–322.

Lieberman, M. A. (1990). A group therapist perspective on self-help groups. *International Journal of Group Psychotherapy, 40*, 251–278.

Lieberman, M. A., & Snowden, L. R. (1994). Problems in assessing prevalence and membership characteristics of self-help group participants. In J. T. Powell (Ed.), *Understanding the self-help organization: Frameworks and findings* (pp. 32–49). Thousand Oaks, CA: Sage.

Lighthouse National Center for Vision and Aging. (1992). *Self-help/mutual aid support groups for visually impaired older people: A guide and directory*. New York: The Lighthouse.

Longino, C. F., & Lipman, A. (1982). The married, the formerly married and the never married: Support system differentials of older women in planned retirement communities. *International Journal of Aging and Human Development, 15*, 285–297.

Lowy, L. (1992). Social group work with elders: Linkages and intergenerational relationships. In J. A. Garland (Ed.), *Group work reaching out: People, places and power*. Binghamton, NY: Haworth Press, Inc.

Lyon, E., & Moore, N. (1990). Social workers and self-help groups for transitional crises: An agency experience. *Social Work with Groups, 13*, 85–99.

Luks, A. (1991). *The helping power of doing good: The health and spiritual benefits of helping others*. New York: Fawcett Columbine.

Maddox, G. L., & Clark, R. L. (1983). Inflation and the economic well-being of older Americans: Experiences of the decade 1970–1980 (Center Reports on Advances in Research 7). Durham, NC: Duke University Center for the Study of Aging and Human Development.

Maton, K. (1988). Social support, organizational characteristics, psychological well-being, and group appraisal in three self-help group populations. *American Journal of Community Psychology, 16*, 53–88.

Medvene, L. J. (1990). Family support organizations: The functions of similarity. In T. J. Powell (Ed.), *Working with self-help* (pp. 120–140). Silver Spring, MD: NASW Press.

Mercer, S. O. (1994). Navajo elders in a reservation nursing home: Health status profile. *Journal of Gerontological Social Work, 23*, 3–29.

Mettler, M., & Kemper, D. W. (1993). Self-care and older adults: Making healthcare relevant. *Generations, Fall,* 7–10.

Mockenhaupt, R. (1993). Self-care for older adults: Taking care and taking charge. *Generations, Fall,* 5–6.

Moon, M. (1985). *Poverty among elderly women and minorities.* Unpublished discussion paper, Urban Institute, Washington, DC.

Mulligan, K. (1996). Heilbrunian adventures: Embrace challenges of midlife, spirited writer, scholar tells women. *AARP Bulletin, 37,* 16.

Nager, N., & McGowan, T. (1994). Elder care: The employee benefit of the 1990s. *Compensation and Benefits Management, 10,* 44–48.

Nash, K. B., & Kramer, K. D. (1994). Self-help for sickle cell disease in African-American communities. In T. J. Powell (Ed.), *Understanding the self-help organization: Frameworks and findings* (pp. 212–226). Thousand Oaks, CA: Sage.

National Policy and Resource Center on Women and Aging. (1995, November). Social Security: A crucial lifeline for women. *The Women & Aging Newsletter, 1,* 1.

Norburn, J. E. K., Bernard, S. L., Konrad, T. R., Woomert, A., DeFriese, G. H., Kalsbeek, W. D., Koch, G. G., & Ory, M. G. (1995). Self-care and assistance from others in coping with functional status limitations among a national sample of older adults. *Journal of Gerontology: Social Sciences, 50B,* S101–S109.

O'Grady-LeShane, R. (1990). Older women and poverty. *Social Work, 35,* 422–424.

Ott, R. L. (1993). Enhancing validation through milestoning with sensory reminiscence. *Journal of Gerontological Social Work, 20,* 147–159.

Ozawa, M. N. (1995). The economic status of vulnerable older women. *Social Work, 40,* 323–331.

Perkins, K. P. (1990). *Blue collar women and retirement.* Unpublished doctoral dissertation, University of Pennsylvania.

Perkins, K. P. (1992). Psychosocial implications of women and retirement. *Social Work, 37,* 526–532.

Powell, T. J. (1987). *Self-help organizations and professional practice.* Silver Spring, MD: National Association of Social Workers.

Powell, T. J. (Ed.). (1990). *Working with self-help.* Silver Spring, MD: NASW Press.

Powell, T. J. (1994). *Understanding the self-help organization: Frameworks and findings.* Thousand Oaks, CA: Sage.

Preston, S. H. (1984). Children and the elderly: Divergent paths for America's dependents. *Demography, 21,* 435–457.

Rakowski, W., Julius, M., Hickey, T., & Halter, J. B. (1987). Correlates of preventive health behaviors in late life. *Research on Aging, 9,* 331–355.

Regier, D. A., Boyd, J. H., Burke, J. D., Rae, D. S., Myers, J. K., Kramer, M., Ronbins, L. N., George, L. K., Karno, M., & Locke, B. Z. (1988). One-month prevalence of mental disorders in the United States. *Archives of General Psychiatry, 45,* 977–986.

Rheingold, H. (1993). *The virtual community: Homesteading on the electronic frontier.* Reading, MA: Addison-Wesley.

Rice, F. (1994). Menopause and the working boomer. *Fortune, 130,* 203–212.

Riessman, F., & Carroll, D. (1995). *Redefining self-help: Policy and practice.* San Francisco, CA: Jossey-Bass.

Rife, J. C., Toomey, B. G., & First, R. J. (1989). Older women's adjustment to unemployment. *Affilia: Journal of Women and Social Work, 4*, 65–77.

Roberto, K. A., & Scott, J. P. (1984). Friendship patterns among older women. *International Journal of Aging and Human Development, 19*, 1–10.

Rodeheaver, D. (1987). The helper-therapy principle. *Social Work, 10*, 27–32.

Rybarczyk, B. (1995). Using reminiscence interviews for stress management in the medical setting. In B. K. Haight & J. D. Webster (Eds.), *The art and science of reminiscing: Theory, research, methods, and applications.* Washington, DC: Taylor & Francis.

Salzer, M. S., McFadden, L., & Rappaport, J. (1994). Professional views of self-help groups. *Administration and Policy in Mental Health, 22*, 85–95.

Sanchez-Ayendez, M. (1988). Puerto Rican elderly women: The cultural dimension of social support networks. *Women and Health, 14*, 239–252.

Snowden, L. R., & Lieberman, M. A. (1994). African-American participation in self-help groups. In T. J. Powell (Ed.), *Understanding the self-help organization: Frameworks and findings* (pp. 50–61). Thousand Oaks, CA: Sage.

The Society for the Advancement of Women's Health. (1991). *Toward a women's health research agenda.* Washington, DC: Author.

Staight, P. R., & Harvey, S. M. (1990). Caregiver burden: A comparison between elderly women as primary and secondary caregivers for their spouses. *Journal of Gerontological Social Work, 15*, 89–104.

Suler, J. (1984). The role of ideology in self-help groups. *Social Policy, 14*, 29–36.

Supportive Older Women's Network. (1992). *The power of support: A guide for creating self-help support groups for older women.* Philadelphia, PA: Supportive Older Women's Network.

Szinovacz, M. (1986). Preferred retirement planning and retirement satisfaction in women. *International Journal of Aging and Human Development, 24*, 301–317.

Tanjasiri, S. P., Wallace, S. P., & Shibata, K. (1995). Picture imperfect: Hidden problems among Asian Pacific Islander elderly. *The Gerontologist, 35*, 753–760.

Tarnowski, D. L. (1996). *Reminiscence therapy as an intervention strategy with the depressed elderly in a partial hospital setting.* Bryn Mawr, PA: Graduate School of Social Work & Social Research, Bryn Mawr College.

Taueber, C. (1993). *Nursing home population: 1990* (Listings CPH-L-137). Washington, DC: U.S. Bureau of the Census.

Thorsheim, H. I., & Roberts, B. (1995). Finding common ground and mutual social support through reminiscing and telling one's story. In B. K. Haight & J. D. Webster (Eds.), *The art and science of reminiscing: Theory, research, methods, and applications.* Washington, DC: Taylor & Francis.

Toseland, R. W. (1995). *Group work with the elderly and family caregivers.* New York: Springer.

Toseland, R., & Hacker, L. (1982). Self-help groups and professional involvement. *Social Work, 27*, 341–347.

Toseland, R. W., Rossiter, C. M., & Labreque, M. S. (1989). The effectiveness of peer-led and professionally led groups to support family caregivers. *The Gerontologist, 29*, 465–471.

United Nations. (1990). *Demographic yearbook: 1988.* New York: United Nations.

U.S. Bureau of the Census. (1970, March). *1970 current population survey*. Unpublished data.

U.S. Bureau of the Census. (1991). *Statistical abstract of the United States: 1991*. Washington, DC: United States Government Printing Office.

U.S. Bureau of the Census. (1992a, March). *Current population survey*. Unpublished data.

U.S. Bureau of the Census. (1992b). *Marital status and living arrangements: March 1992*, Current Population Reports (Series P20-468). Washington, DC: U.S. Government Printing Office.

U.S. Bureau of the Census. (1993a). Current population reports (Series P25-1104). Washington, DC: U.S. Government Printing Office.

U.S. Bureau of the Census. (1993b, March). *1993 current population survey*. Unpublished data.

U.S. Bureau of the Census. (1993c, November and December). *1993 current population survey*. Unpublished data.

U.S. Bureau of the Census. (1993d, September). *Poverty in the United States: 1992* (Current Population Reports, Series P60-185). Washington, DC: U.S. Government Printing Office.

U.S. Bureau of the Census. (1993e, November). *Supplement to the American housing survey for the United States in 1991* (Current Housing Reports, Series H 151/91). Washington, DC: U.S. Government Printing Office.

U.S. National Center for Health Statistics. (1993). Vital statistics of the United States (annual). Washington, D.C.: U.S. Government Printing Office.

Verbrugge, L. M. (1983). Longer life but worsening health: Trends in health and morbidity of middle-aged and older men and women. *Milbank Memorial Fund Quarterly, 62*, 475–519.

Verbrugge, L. M. (1985). Gender and health: An update on hypotheses and evidence. *Journal of Health and Social Behavior, 26*, 156–182.

Videka-Sherman, L. (1990). Bereavement self-help organizations. In T. J. Powell (Ed.), *Working with self-help* (pp. 156–174). Silver Spring, MD: NASW Press.

Villers Foundation. (1987). *On the other side of easy street: Myths & facts about the economics of old age*. Washington, DC: Author.

Vinick, B. H., & Ekerdt, D. J. (1989). Retirement and the family. *Generations, 13*, 53–56.

Wachel, W. (1992). As they see it: Experts forecast trends and challenges. *Healthcare Executive, 7*, 16–20.

Wachtel, T. J., & Stein, M. D. (1995). HIV infection in older persons. In W. Reichel (Ed.), *Care of the elderly: Clinical aspects of aging* (4th ed.). Baltimore: Williams & Wilkins.

Wellman, B. (1981). Applying network analysis to the study of support. In B. H. Gottlieb (Ed.), *Social networks and social support* (pp. 171–200). Beverly Hills, CA: Sage.

Wilson, P. A., Moore, S. T., Rubin, D. S., & Bartels, P. K. (1990). Informal caregivers of the chronically ill and their social support: A pilot study. *Journal of Gerontological Social Work, 15*, 155–170.

Wilson, V. (1990). The consequences of elderly wives caring for disabled husbands: Implications for practice. *Social Work, 35*, 417–421.

Woroby, J. L., & Angel, R. J. (1990). Poverty and health: Older minority women and the rise of the female-headed household. *Journal of Health and Social Behavior, 31*, 370–383.

Zultowski, W. H. (1995). Finding tomorrow's agents: Embrace change now or later. *Managers Magazine, 70*, 12–14.

Appendix A

Techniques Used to Analyze Project Information and Determine Representativeness of Project Participants

This section includes additional detail concerning the specific procedures used (a) to analyze information collected during the various phases of the project and (b) to determine the representativeness of the older women affiliated with SOWN who agreed to participate in the project.

ANALYTIC PROCEDURES

Quantitative computer analysis of self-help group member and facilitator survey data (chapters 4–7) combined with both quantitative and qualitative analysis of data from the field and telephone interviews with group members and facilitators (chapters 4–7), the self-help expert panel (chapter 8), and study site staff (chapters 4–7) were performed. Descriptive statistics and measures of association were used where appropriate on the group member database (chapters 4–7), including chi-squares, Pearson correlation coefficients, t tests, univariate analyses of variance, and multivariate analyses (e.g., multiple regression). The small number of individuals composing the group facilitator sample considerably limited the extent of analysis of this data source.

A new dependent variable was constructed as an additional means of assessing program impact. The Gain Through Group Involvement Scale, also presented in chapter 7, measures the extent to which members felt they realized personal gain in various areas of social and emotional functioning as a result of involvement in SOWN. This 15-item index is scored on a 15-point scale in which 0 = *no aspects of social and emotional functioning reported gained from SOWN membership* and 15 = *15 areas of social and emotional functioning reported gained*. Thus, the score is equivalent to the number of areas of functioning that respondents reported that they had gained through SOWN membership. The higher the score on this scale, the more the respondent felt she had gained as a result of her SOWN group experience. The social and emotional functioning items included in the scale are listed below:

- new friendships
- listening to others better

- what to do when I feel lonely
- handling the blues
- handling stress better
- facing issues about death and loss
- dealing with family relationships
- finding health care
- support for being an older woman
- valuing the past
- awareness about how myths and stereotypes affect my self-image
- support for being me
- new sense of accomplishment
- self-confidence
- how to say *yes* and *no*

The index mean and standard deviation were 5.21 and 3.39, respectively. Thus, the average woman indicated that she had realized personal gain in slightly more than five areas of social and emotional functioning. The standardized item alpha for this scale was .79, reflecting a moderate level of reliability or internal index item consistency.

COMPARATIVE ANALYSIS
OF RESPONDENTS AND NONRESPONDENTS

To determine whether those SOWN members who answered questionnaires ($N = 225$) were representative of all SOWN members, a telephone survey of nonrespondents was undertaken. Survey participants were asked a selected set of demographic questions including ones regarding their age, marital status, race, years of education, employment or volunteer status, and health status. Furthermore, they were asked about the length of their membership in SOWN, their attendance rate, and their intentions regarding continued SOWN membership.

Of 77 questionnaire nonrespondents randomly chosen with replacement from a master list of SOWN members (20% of the total population), 25 members participated in the telephone survey, resulting in a response rate of 32.5%. Respondents and nonrespondents did not vary significantly except in terms of their self-reported health status. Nonrespondents were significantly more likely to report poorer health. Other data reflecting membership intentions serve also to confirm that nonrespondents were more likely to state that they were no longer involved with a SOWN group. Thus, participants in our analysis were likely to be healthier and to have remained involved in SOWN programming. These differences in the profiles of participants and nonparticipants should be considered in interpreting the results of the analysis of SOWN questionnaire data.

Appendix B

Where to Turn for Information

The process of developing a self-help organization for older women, or even expanding the scope or membership of an existing program, can be facilitated by using available resources. There are many associations, books, and manuals designed as guides to establishing and implementing a self-help group, and others can provide assistance by offering subject matter related to the group's central topic. Certain established self-help organizations, such as SOWN, can serve as models for similar organizations and programs in the earlier phases of development. The International Society for Retirement Planning, among others, offers presentations and materials that may be appropriate for certain self-help groups.

The following sampling of resources is by no means intended to be an exhaustive listing. Rather, it offers a representative sample of useful sources of information as a starting point in the creation or expansion of a self-help organization for older women. The resources below will, in addition, direct you to yet other related sources.

BOOKS, MANUALS, AND NEWSLETTERS

Aging Well: A Guide for Successful Seniors. J. Fries. Reading, MA: Addison-Wesley, 1989.

Healthwise for Life: Medical Self-Care for Healthy Aging. M. Mettler & D. W. Kemper. Boise, ID: Healthwise, 1992.

Organizing a Self-Help Clearinghouse. L. Borck & E. Aronowitz. New York: National Self-Help Clearinghouse, 1981.

Surgeon General's Workshop on Self-Help and Public Health. U.S. Department of Health and Human Services. Washington, DC: U.S. Government Printing Office, 1987.

Taking Care of Today and Tomorrow: A Resource Guide for Health, Aging and Long-Term Care. The Center for Corporate Health. Reston, VA: Author, 1991.

The Power of Support: A Guide for Creating Self-Help Support Groups for Older Women (2nd ed.). Merle Drake and the Supportive Older Women's Network. Philadelphia: SOWN, 1993. (See also Organizations.)

The Self-Help Resource Kit: Training Materials to Enhance Professional Support of Support Groups. J. Cardinal & A. Farquharson. Victoria, British Columbia, Canada: University of Victoria, 1991.

The Self-Help Sourcebook. E. Madara & B. White (Eds.). Denville, NJ: St. Clair's–Riverside Medical Center, 1992.

The Self-Help Sourcebook: Finding and Forming Mutual Aid Self-Help Groups (2nd ed.). E. Madara & A. Meese (Eds.). Denville, NJ: New Jersey Self-Help Clearinghouse, 1988.

Women and Aging Letter. Published by the National Policy and Resource Center on Women and Aging. Contact: Editorial Office, Heller School MS 035, Brandeis University, Waltham, MA 02254-9110. (800) 929-1995.

SELF-HELP GROUPS, ORGANIZATIONS, AND INTEREST GROUPS

Center for Self-Help Research & Knowledge Dissemination
University of Michigan
1239 Kipke Drive
Ann Arbor, Michigan 48109
(313) 764-1817

Daughters of the Elderly Bringing the Unknown Together (DEBUT)
710 Concord Street
Ellettsville, Indiana 47429
(812) 876-5319

Grandparents as Caregivers Interest Group
Gerontological Society of America
Brookdale Foundation Group
126 East 56th Street
New York, New York 10023
(212) 308-7355

Institute on Mutual Aid/Self-Help
Brookdale Foundation Group
126 E. 56th Street
New York, New York 10023
(212) 308-7355

National Self-Help Clearinghouse
City University of New York Graduate
School & University Center
25 West 43rd Street
Room 620
New York, New York 10036
(212) 642-2944

Self-Help Center
405 South State Street
Champaign, Illinois 61820
(217) 352-0099

Self-Help Clearinghouse
75 Market Street
Poughkeepsie, New York 12601
(914) 473-1500

Self-Help Clearinghouse
184 Salem Avenue
Dayton, Ohio 45402
(513) 225-3004

Self-Help Mental Health Research Center
University of Michigan
1239 Kipke Drive
Ann Arbor, Michigan 48109
(313) 764-1817

Self-Help Network of Kansas
Wichita State University
RR 1
Viola, Kansas 67149
(316) 584-6626

Supportive Older Women's Network (SOWN)
2805 North 47th Street
Philadelphia, Pennsylvania 19131
(215) 477-6000

Women's Issues Interest Group
Gerontological Society of America
Kino Community Hospital
Department of Pharmaceutical Services
2800 East Ajo Way
Tucson, Arizona 85713
(520) 741-6949

Women's Self-Help Center
2838 Olive Street
St. Louis, Missouri 63103
(314) 531-9100

Women's Self-Help Center, Inc.
341 East E Street
Casper, Wyoming 82601
(307) 235-2814

RELATED ORGANIZATIONS AND PROGRAMS

AARP Women's Initiative
AARP
601 E Street, NW
Washington, DC 20049
(202) 434-2400

Ensures that the economic, social, health, and long-term care needs of midlife and older women are met. Advocates and supports policies, programs, and legislation that improve the status of women.

Alzheimer's Disease and Related Disorders Association, Inc.
360 North Michigan Avenue
Chicago, Illinois 60601
(800) 272-3900

Raises public awareness of the problem of Alzheimer's disease and generates funds for basic research. Provides support group referrals and educational materials.

American Association for International Aging
1133 20th Street NW, Suite 330
Washington, DC 20036
(202) 833-8893

Seeks to improve the socioeconomic conditions of older, low-income persons in developing countries through self-help, mutual support, and economic development.

American Health Assistance Foundation
15825 Shady Grove Road
Suite 140
Rockville, Maryland 20850
(800) 437-2423

Offers training and educational resources on health and wellness promotion.

American Parkinson's Disease Association
47 East 50th Street, Room 602
New York, New York 10022
(212) 598-6300

Raises public understanding of and offers educational materials on Parkinson's disease.

Arthritis Foundation
67 Irving Place
New York, New York 10003
(212) 477-8700

Provides information on coping with arthritis.

Elder-Health
School of Pharmacy
University of Maryland
20 North Pine Street
Baltimore, Maryland 21201
(301) 405-2273

A joint project of Parke-Davis Center for the Education of the Elderly, Elder-Health Program, University of Maryland, and the Elder-Care Program. Provides educational materials to older adults concerning medication use, personal health care, and health care planning.

Healthwise for Life: A Self-Care Workshop and Handbook
Healthwise
P.O. Box 1989
Boise, Idaho 83701
(208) 345-1161

An interactive, 2-hour workshop encouraging older adults to be more active participants in their medical care. Both live and videotaped versions are available as well as a handbook and program materials. Available through Healthwise, whose mission is to help people stay healthy by taking care of their health matters.

International Menopause Society
c/o Monique Boulet
116, Avenue de Broqueville
Bte. 9
B-1200 Brussels, Belgium
(2) 7719598

Promotes study of medical, sociological, and psychological aspects of menopause. Provides publications in English.

International Society for Retirement Planning
833 Market Street, Suite 511
San Francisco, California 94103-1824
(415) 974-9631

Acts as a clearinghouse on common methods, techniques, materials, devices, and content used in preretirement programs. Holds presentations on topics including women and retirement. Offers reduced rates on books and free copies of materials.

National Hispanic Council on Aging
2713 Ontario Road NW
Washington, DC 20009
(202) 265-1288

Fosters the well-being of Hispanic elderly through research, policy analysis, development of educational programs, and training. Provides a network and speakers' bureau for organizations interested in the Hispanic elderly.

National Policy and Resource Center on Women and Aging
Heller School MS 035
Brandeis University
Waltham, Massachusetts 02254-9110
(800) 929-1995

A project of Brandeis University, the American Society on Aging, the National Black Women's Health Project, and the Coalition of Labor Union Women. Produces the Women and Aging Letter.

Ohlone Older Women's League (OOWL)
1041 Talbot Avenue
Albany, California 94701
(510) 527-7923

Serves middle-aged and older women in the East Bay area of California. Promotes equity for members in employment, health care, and housing.

Older Women's League (OWL)
666 11th Street NW, Suite 700
Washington, DC 20001
(202) 783-6686

Offers in-depth information on women and retirement.

Senior Healthtrac
525 Middlefield Road
Suite 250
Menlo Park, California 94025
(415) 324-1749

A comprehensive self-care health promotion and disease prevention program designed to lower health risk by increasing health life-style behaviors. Includes self-care education.

The Arthritis Self-Management Program (ASMP)
Contact any local chapter of the Arthritis Foundations in
the United States and Australia and the Arthritis
Society in Canada
(800) 283-7800 (for local chapter information in the United States)

A 12-hour course offered over a 6-week period in community locations such as senior centers, libraries, and churches. Courses are attended by people with arthritis and taught by trained lay leaders who often have arthritis themselves.

Women in An Ageing Society
P.O. Box 1078
Cochrane, Alberta, Canada T0L 0W0
(403) 932-6584

Works to enhance the social and economic well-being of older women in Canada. Promotes public awareness of the skills and capabilities of older women.

Index

Advocacy
  long-term care, 52
  self-help groups and, 19–20
African American women
  attendance at religious functions,
    17
  financial status, 12
  health and mortality rate, 13
  participation in self-help groups,
    23–24, 91, 119
  vs. Whites in SOWN, 44
Age
  definition of old, 1–2
  effect on self-help group's
    perception, 18
  self-help group's content and, 101
  served by self-help groups, 91,
    123
Aging, women and challenge of,
  30–31
AIDS, 6
Asian-Pacific Islander women
  health and mortality rate, 14
  income, 13
  participation in self-help groups,
    91

Breast cancer, 6

Caregiver
  description of typical, 3
  elderly women as, 3–4
Chronic disorder, 6
Community, sense of, self-help groups
  and, 19
Coping strategies, self-help groups
  and teaching of, 19–20
Counseling services, 52

Dependency risk, 3
Depression, 6
Diversity, effects of group, 70–71
Divorce, later-life, 4

Education
  satisfaction from self-help programs
    and level of, 78, 119
  self-help programs and community,
    50–51
  SOWN members', 46–47
Elders Health Program, 22
Emotional changes
  group helpfulness to members
    during, 79–81, 121
  SOWN members, 46
Employment, minority women, 13
Empowerment, SOWN and women,
  50–51

Facilitator
  challenges for peer, 95–96, 119–120
  characteristics of self-help groups'
    peer, 38
  group's influence on, 75–76
  group's topic and, 100
  members' support for, 119
  perception of leadership role, 72–74
  perspectives on members' needs,
    59
  profile of peer group, 118
  profile of SOWN group, 47–48
  quality of experience, 67–68
  role of, 95
  selection of, 108
  socializing with members, 68–69
  training of group, 54–55, 124–125
  views of group meeting, 58